Office K

Transforming Office Operations into a Strategic Competitive Advantage

Also available from ASQ Quality Press:

The Trust Imperative: Performance Improvement through Productive Relationships
Stephen Hacker and Marsha Willard

Root Cause Analysis: Simplified Tools and Techniques
Bjørn Andersen and Tom Fagerhaug

Six Sigma Project Management: A Pocket Guide
Jeffrey N. Lowenthal

Six Sigma for the Shop Floor: A Pocket Guide
Roderick A. Munro

The Change Agent's Guide to Radical Improvement
Ken Miller

Customer Centered Six Sigma: Linking Customers, Process Improvement, and Financial Results
Earl Naumann and Steven H. Hoisington

Lean Enterprise: A Synergistic Approach to Minimizing Waste
William A. Levinson and Raymond A. Rerick

Managing Change: Practical Strategies for Competitive Advantage
Kari Tuominen

The Certified Quality Manager Handbook, Second Edition
Duke Okes and Russell T. Westcott

To request a complimentary catalog of ASQ Quality Press publications, call 800-248-1946, or visit our Web site at http://qualitypress.asq.org .

Office Kaizen

Transforming Office Operations into a Strategic Competitive Advantage

William Lareau

ASQ Quality Press
Milwaukee, Wisconsin

Office Kaizen: Transforming Office Operations into a Strategic Competitive Advantage
William Lareau

Library of Congress Cataloging-in-Publication Data

Lareau, William.
  Office kaizen : transforming office operations into a strategic competitive advantage / William Lareau.
    p. cm.
  Includes bibliographical references and index.
  ISBN 0-87389-556-8
  1. Organizational change. 2. Industrial efficiency. 3. Corporate culture. 4. Competition. I. Title.

  HD58.8 .L373 2002
  658.4'06—dc21   2002008313

10 9 8 7 6 5 4 3 2

ISBN 0-87389-556-8

Acquisitions Editor: Annemieke Koudstaal
Project Editor: Craig S. Powell
Production Administrator: Gretchen Trautman
Special Marketing Representative: David Luth

ASQ Mission: The American Society for Quality advances individual, organizational, and community excellence worldwide through learning, quality improvement, and knowledge exchange.

Attention Bookstores, Wholesalers, Schools, and Corporations: ASQ Quality Press books, videotapes, audiotapes, and software are available at quantity discounts with bulk purchases for business, educational, or instructional use. For information, please contact ASQ Quality Press at 800-248-1946, or write to ASQ Quality Press, P.O. Box 3005, Milwaukee, WI 53201-3005.

To place orders or to request a free copy of the ASQ Quality Press Publications Catalog, including ASQ membership information, call 800-248-1946. Visit our Web site at www.asq.org or http://qualitypress.asq.org .

Printed in the United States of America

∞ Printed on acid-free paper

American Society for Quality

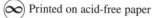

ASQ

Quality Press
600 N. Plankinton Avenue
Milwaukee, Wisconsin 53203
Call toll free 800-248-1946
Fax 414-272-1734
www.asq.org
http://qualitypress.asq.org
http://standardsgroup.asq.org
E-mail: authors@asq.org

Table of Contents

Acknowledgments

I have been privileged to work with an outstanding group of colleagues in the past six years. They are masters of their craft. Each and every one of them has made significant contributions to my perspectives on applied organization improvement. While I cannot thank them all (due to space and memory limitations), a number of people must be mentioned. Roger Kaufman was the driving force in motivating me to write this book. Jerry Timpson made significant conceptual contributions that I would not have developed without his help. Bob Laux, project manager extraordinaire, has been instrumental in developing my ever-deepening appreciation of structure over the years. Bert Mooney, "the" management mentor, has been a source of insightful perspectives concerning implementation and, in particular, the coaching of executives. Greg Piper, the master of applied implementation, has been a continuing source of practical tips for getting things done in the trenches.

Others who made important contributions include Bill Roper, Will Allen, Andy Herdan, Rob Wagner, Bob McAvoy, Julien Renaud, Jeff Hageness, Colleen Bodvig, and Andy Magee. In particular, Brad Anderson provided insights concerning the structure and organization of the metrics chapter that were exceptional.

Finally, we come to the person that guided this book (and its immediate predecessor, *Lean Leadership*) through the manuscript development process. Along the way, she also made many significant creative contributions (for example, "George" and his entire staff owe their lives to her). She coordinated the input of many reviewers in a constantly changing, ego-involved situation and dealt with it all in a calm and professional manner. She conceived, developed, and produced the cover and book design of the bound galley of *Office Kaizen* (as well as the published version of *Lean Leadership*). This creative dynamo and ego referee is Katherine "Katie" Burt.

William Lareau
West Lafayette, Indiana
April 14, 2002

1

Introduction

"We need to do something different," asserted George, the CEO of Biginslow Corporation, to a conference table of attentive but discomfited executives. "Administration and engineering costs are climbing at a rate faster than sales. Problems with our products go undiscovered until our customers' customers are already using them. Things are fixed, but they don't stay fixed. Our ISO and QS efforts resulted in certified operations that still don't have reliable, standardized processes. Plus, costs for all the programming and customization fixes to the new enterprise information system are now higher than the cost of the new system itself; and we still have reporting errors and bad numbers! Worst of all, our people lack the focus and discipline to get meaningful results from any of the initiatives we institute!"

"Well, who could blame them?" retorted the somewhat exasperated Madison, the VP of Finance. She continued, "Nobody owns anything at the work group level anymore. We have Six Sigma Blackbelts running around, quality teams, ISO committees, benchmarking teams, continuous improvement teams, balanced scorecard committees, communication teams, and reengineering teams, to name a few. Last year, we spent millions of dollars just on travel to get together to compare notes on these corporate-sponsored initiatives! Talk about a lack of focus! We have so many different improvement and quality initiatives that everybody is responsible to everybody else, but nobody has ownership of anything. I'm afraid to get a cup of coffee for fear that somebody will tell me I didn't check with the newly launched 'hot beverage team' or, worse yet, that I've inadvertently created a coup by using the coffee mug from *last* month's improvement effort. If I were a typical employee, I would sit still and wait; because no matter what I did, it would run afoul of some tee-shirted, certificate-granting, coffee-cupped team."

The group laughed. They all had similar thoughts from time to time, but it was an uneasy laugh. Monica, the corporate legal counsel, asked the group, "How about a companywide effort to reengineer our processes and pare down the teams and initiatives at the same time?"

George sat down on the arm of the sofa facing them. "The last thing we need is another 'flavor-of-the-month' reengineering or quality initiative. I've got enough three-ring binders on my bookshelf to start a training institute. And we can't very well just chop all the existing stuff without doing something more value-added. It would send the wrong message. We may not be 100 percent on-target in what we've done, but there's no sense in demoralizing the troops."

He stood up and walked back and forth in front of the window. "No, no, this is a much more fundamental problem. Our people are working hard, but we're not getting what we, as business units and locations, need. Units, departments, and people have objectives that are generally attained, but it seems that we always do it the hard way. We're always recovering from problems or fixing things at the last minute. At times, it seems as though we have sand in our gears."

"Despite the problems, we do make our numbers every year, don't we?" offered Jack, the VP of Operations. "We are number one or two in almost every segment we're in. Maybe we need to look at the front end of the business for improvement of our delivery and cycle times."

"Of course," ventured Emma, the VP of Human Resources, "there's room for improvement in any process, but there's always going to be some slippage in office-based operations. Maybe it's just a fact of corporate life."

George turned away from the window and faced the group. "I can't accept that. I won't accept that. You can't accept that.

There are service companies out there that consist of nothing *but* office operations, and they beat the pants off their competition in service, sales, response time, reputation, and profits year after year after year. For them, office operations themselves are both the product and a competitive advantage. I'm not looking for some quickie five percent cost savings and the elimination of a few embarrassing problems. That won't help our customers very much, and it will be barely visible to our shareholders. More critically, it won't last very long."

"How about a 10 percent across-the-board headcount reduction in Admin and Support to look a little better to the analysts? Just the news of the planned cutbacks would give the stock a shot in the arm," offered Evan, the VP of Sales.

George shook his head. "We don't need an artificial stock hit badly enough to risk the consequences. Besides, we've tried that in the past, and the result is always more screw-ups; plus, we'll alienate our best customers. Good people will leave, and the headcount will creep right back up over the following 18 months. We may be overstaffed. In fact, I'm sure we are in many places; but we'll never resolve the problems by mandating a seniority- or personality-based cut across the company.

"Look, I want our office and support functions to do the same thing for us that they do for world-class service companies. I want them to add to the competitive advantage we've created with manufacturing, not just get dragged along for the ride. I want our front and back office administrative and support functions to be recognized by everyone as major, long-term, visible, and dramatic elements of our success. I want every office function to be a strategic competitive advantage that is feared by our competitors, adored by our customers, and a pleasure for everyone in our own organization to deal with."

George continued, "The way I see it, we all agree to some extent that we have some chronic, bedeviling problems. I also appreciate your honesty in pointing out that these aren't new problems. And as the variety of coffee mugs sitting on this table indicate, we've certainly tried in the past couple of years to address the problems with one initiative after another. It appears to me that we have not been able to sustain our focus, let alone own up to the real problems or solutions. I want to assure our future success and enhance our position!" George looked around the room and seemed to zero in on each person as he said, "Now tell me, what can we do to become an organization that creates a competitive advantage in how it does the work, rather than having to constantly firefight and recover? What can we do to move ourselves away from the pack just because we run our day-to-day business better than anyone has a right to expect?"

The executives looked at each other. They understood exactly what George was talking about. At the same time many were thinking that while it may be possible to have comparatively great office functions, raising them to the level of a strategic competitive advantage seemed, well, almost impossible. And, even if it were possible, not one of them had the slightest idea of how to do it.

Suddenly, the heavy conference room doors swung wide open and in walked George's assistant, Mary, announcing that lunch had arrived. As the group sorted through the various orders with less than their usual vigor, Mary quietly slipped a book in front of George. "What's this?" asked George.

"It arrived today, from Research," replied Mary. George announced a 30-minute break and headed to his office. As he paused in the doorway, he turned and told the group, "Let's try to come up with some ideas to discuss after lunch."

Seated at his coffee table and intrigued by the title, *Office Kaizen: Transforming Office Operations into a Strategic Competitive Advantage*, George began flipping through the pages as he devoured his meatball sandwich. He saw the words "focus" and "structure." "Hmm," he thought, "maybe I'll put off returning phone calls for ten minutes and read a chapter or two."

Almost every executive has had thoughts similar to George's; and, almost every management team has been told that it must begin the first phase of the challenge laid down by George: *dramatically improve office, administrative, and support functions in a consistent, reliable manner that adds value and doesn't create more problems.* The difficulty is that few management teams have ever dramatically improved an office or administrative function from fair to good, much less turned it into a strategic competitive weapon.

It seems to many that office and administrative functions just aren't keeping up with the rest of the business world when it comes to contributing more to the bottom line. The technology delivered to customers has improved exponentially in the past 50 years. New products have infinitely better quality at lower constant dollar costs. Products work better and last longer. Services provided to businesses and individuals (such as insurance, loans, package delivery, airline e-tickets, car rentals, e-mail, mobile phone service, and the like) are dramatically cheaper, faster, and easier to use than their counterparts were 20 years ago.

At the same time, enlightened manufacturing operations are pursuing lean (flexible, synchronous, pull, and so on) techniques that dramatically increase output, decrease inventory, and shorten lead times by factors of two to 10 (or more). Yet, despite expensive technology of every type and computers on every desk, office and administrative operations have not kept pace. Office costs per unit of product hardly ever decrease without compromising service levels. It sometimes seems as if office functions, even in highly competitive organizations, operate in a disjointed, slightly off-kilter world that is disconnected from the flinty, exacting demands of today's marketplaces by a gossamer veil of phones, computers, cubicles, and endless meetings.

Office Kaizen* creates office and administrative processes and work groups that generate a competitive advantage, not compromise it. Competitive advantage will come from several simultaneous fronts. There will be significant cost decreases and performance increases (fewer errors, faster cycle time, and so on) across all office and administrative functions. There will be increased precision in planning and financial analyses, because better data will be available faster. Additional competitive advantage will come from the increased support these office areas will provide for manufacturing and engineering. Good designs and good factories will be given a leg up to become even better—something they cannot do if they are not supported by world-class office functions.

The word *kaizen* is a compound Japanese word. "Kai" means "little," "ongoing," and "good." "Zen" means "for the better" and "good." It is pronounced "k-eye-zen." The word has become part of the Toyota Production System (TPS), where it means "small, continuous improvements on everyone's part." In spite of the association of the word "kaizen" with the TPS, be assured that Office Kaizen is not a translation of the TPS to the office environment. Such simplistic applications are off the mark, work poorly, and would not get to the root of the "office problem."

If it were not for the necessity of establishing a unique identity for Office Kaizen, it could just as easily be called Office Continuous Improvement, Office Innovation/Change Management, Office Productivity

---

*Office Kaizen is a service mark of The Kaufman Consulting Group, LLC.

Improvement, Office Cost Control, Office Project Management, Office Right-sizing Management, or all of these names. In fact, insofar as Office Kaizen implies all of the above, any *one* of the above names would be too restrictive to be accurate. At the same time, all of the elements of Office Kaizen, with minor changes of names, mesh perfectly with and support any and all well–thought out process improvement methodologies. This is because Office Kaizen is a method for providing structure, focus, discipline, and ownership to any initiative or system run by human beings. Office Kaizen will smoothly support and dramatically improve the effectiveness of any continuous improvement effort, project, or work group, because Office Kaizen is based upon fundamental truths about people, processes, and business.

There are literally hundreds of theories about leadership and management. Almost all of them present two severe problems for executives:

1. They do not relate to the real world. The concepts are
   intellectually interesting but deal with many issues that
   are difficult to assess, control, and/or manipulate in a
   functioning organization.

2. They do not specify the exact, concrete actions that must be
   performed to obtain the claimed improvements when back
   on the job.

Office Kaizen does not suffer from either of these limitations. First of all, Office Kaizen is an approach that establishes a system to reduce waste over the long term. This creates a strategic competitive advantage. There is no theory involved other than the basic realities and facts about people, processes, and waste. Second, Office Kaizen specifies *exactly* what must be done in order to apply the system to an organization (or part of it).

The first step is understanding Office Kaizen and thereby believing in its validity. This understanding is important for two reasons. To lead this change, one will have to coach and "sell" others on its merits. Further, Office Kaizen must be customized to each unique environment. That is, while this book describes exactly what to do, leaders are going to have to make adjustments to fit the "standard" Office Kaizen approach into their organizations. This requires important judgment calls on everyone's part (carefully coached, of course). The only good judgment call is one based upon knowledge. Therefore, leaders must have a fairly comprehensive understanding of "why" and "how" the elements of Office Kaizen operate to produce results.

"Office" implies any business process and function that is not a pure "factory" task, such as assembling, welding, machining, forklift driving, and so on. A number of the functions that Office Kaizen addresses are shown in Figure 1.1.

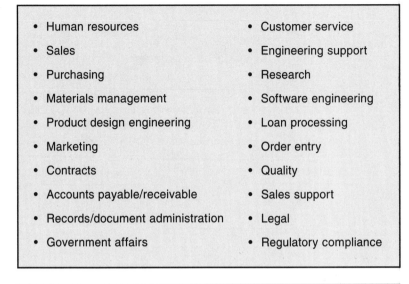

- Human resources
- Sales
- Purchasing
- Materials management
- Product design engineering
- Marketing
- Contracts
- Accounts payable/receivable
- Records/document administration
- Government affairs

- Customer service
- Engineering support
- Research
- Software engineering
- Loan processing
- Order entry
- Quality
- Sales support
- Legal
- Regulatory compliance

Figure 1.1   Representative functions addressed by Office Kaizen.

As Figure 1.1 demonstrates, Office Kaizen relates to almost every aspect of business. In fact, a great deal of the work—even within manufacturing and operations—is devoted to tasks such as paperwork, planning, supervision, benchmarking, and communications that are not "pure" factory tasks. Thus, Office Kaizen applies to both the non-factory elements of "the factory" and to almost everything else that happens in business.

In short, Office Kaizen provides the foundation for the next great, stepwise competitive advantage. Office Kaizen is an implementation path, management philosophy, leadership structure, and set of tools, all wrapped into one consistent package. If employed as an executive-level, strategic weapon across an organization, Office Kaizen will create a competitive advantage that competitors cannot match, unless they do the same thing at the same time. Few will, as most will continue to search for the "brass ring" without realizing the merry-go-round has slowed to a near stop. Those who do not embrace Office Kaizen will be left in the dust of those who do.

The following chapters will pull together the fundamentals of Office Kaizen and rapidly show the benefits that are there for the taking. Miracle? Close to it. The difference is miracles just happen; success generally has to be planned and earned. Office Kaizen ensures success through focus, structure, discipline, and ownership.

2

What Is Office Kaizen and What Does It Do? A "Ten Thousand Foot" View

"An Office Kaizen miracle—sounds too good to be true," thought George, who was somewhat interested in the book's claims but still skeptical, for all programs sound great in concept. He remembered the disasters caused by the poorly run quality circles back in 1984. TQM, benchmarking, and SPC didn't fare much better. Would Office Kaizen amount to the same elaborate set of smoke and mirrors?

Most executives want to know if a concept contains enough "meat" to justify the investment of their time. They do not want to be misled by promises of sirloin only to discover in mid-meal that it is all soy and sawdust. Office Kaizen is pure, 100 percent, grain-fed, prime, aged filet mignon by the ton. Office Kaizen will transform an organization to world-class status if fully embraced. Short of that level of commitment, Office Kaizen provides a variety of leadership methods and management approaches that can be quickly employed on a smaller scale to tremendous gain. Office Kaizen will return the valuable investment of the time required to learn it and install it at least one hundredfold within two months.

Office Kaizen is a leadership philosophy, a management methodology, and a set of tools all wrapped into one. Office Kaizen creates a work environment that is characterized by the following description:

- A highly productive, well-led, informed, and enthusiastic organization . . .

- . . . adept at rapidly implementing required small and large changes while . . .

- . . . continually improving key processes that are fast, results-driven, accurate, repeatable, customer-focused, value-added, aligned with organization goals, scrubbed of waste, and supported and driven by accurate, timely metrics . . .

- . . . in order to provide a strategic competitive advantage.

Office Kaizen is *not*, and does not contain or promote any:

- Rehashed ideas with a new name

- Off-the-wall approaches dreamed up by academics

- Team-building adventures in the woods

- Exhortations that restate the obvious (for example, "Leadership is key!")

- Proprietary training programs that cost an arm and a leg

- Lame, obvious advice (for example, "Cut unnecessary costs!")

- Gimmicks

- Leadership lessons from ancient warriors (for example, "Feel your inner Mongol!")

Office Kaizen does not purport to solve all problems, nor does it promise to "run your business." Planning, strategizing, selling, recruiting, marketing, purchasing, and providing services and products are all challenges of doing business. Business is a level playing field, and how well one deals with these normal business challenges greatly influences the success of the organization. Better planning or recruiting may pull an organization above the constantly roiling surface of its industry's level playing field for a while, but competitors will ultimately copy the improvement or counterbalance the advantage with improvements in other areas. Business combat today is conducted by means of small, short-term advances and setbacks. If an organization can do enough good things better than the competition for a sufficient period of time, it holds itself above the level playing field and, as a result, will make more money for itself and its shareholders. Office Kaizen assures that a very large part of an organization is permanently lifted a significant distance above the level playing field on which it competes.

OFFICE KAIZEN IS NOT A NEW CONCEPT

The problem for the executive striving to pull their organization away from the pack is that everybody is doing the same thing. Any executive who regularly reads *The Economist, The Financial Times, Business Week, Fortune, Forbes,* or *Industry Week* knows what the usual answers are. There are few bold, new ideas that can lift an organization above its industry's playing field for long. Even when an organization comes up with a fresh idea or technology ahead of the competition, there is always the chance that someone else will move faster or more efficiently. Perhaps the most prominent example of this occurrence is Xerox's failure to exploit the amazing concepts that gushed from its Palo Alto Research Center and which others used to launch the personal computer industry.

Office Kaizen lifts an entire organization's performance above the playing field in its industry by enabling the organization to consistently and reliably perform all functions and processes at improved levels of customer service, profit, quality, cycle time, and costs. This improvement is accomplished by requiring all levels of leadership to lead with more focus, structure, discipline, and ownership. Office Kaizen leadership improves everything in the organization by a small but incredibly significant degree. An organization doesn't have to be 100 percent better overnight to be world class; as any world-class organization will attest, the journey to excellence is built upon a succession of very small, maintained improvements in a great many areas, over a long period of time. Office Kaizen is a strategic weapon, because in making everything a little better all the time, it provides an advantage that others don't even consider.

Office Kaizen also enables organizations to be more successful in implementing any bold, new ideas that it *does* pursue. Product and service introductions are completed on time and within budget, and there are very few last-minute firefighting drills. Technological innovations are implemented more smoothly, because Office Kaizen engages and focuses employees to bridge the gap between people and technology. With Office Kaizen, leadership is freed from pursuing quick fixes, short-term competitive advantages, and having to deal with the nagging problems caused by poorly functioning processes at all levels. This provides leadership with critical time to do its real job: lead, plan, strategize, and think.

Office Kaizen provides a powerful, strategic competitive advantage that few organizations will pursue. Bits and pieces of it can be found almost everywhere, but because it cannot be purchased "off-the-shelf" or easily copied, it is not systematically applied by more than one organization in a thousand. Office Kaizen must be installed on-site by a committed and strongly led leadership team. While the components are standard, the installation is always custom. It is this customization to the processes, culture, people, ongoing operations, and priorities of an organization that makes it impossible to "snap" Office Kaizen into place.

Most executives, conditioned over the years to the allure of traditional bold, new ideas, continue to look for the magic bullet of competitiveness in technology, reorganizations, and cost cutting. If they find anything that works, everyone else copies it; some poorly, some well. The end result, after some slight perturbations, is the same old level playing field and continued, frenzied searches for the next magic bullet while their organizations struggle in demoralization, confusion, and inefficiency.

MANAGEMENT'S "BLIND SPOT"

Elimination of wastes is the fundamental, bottom-line, measurable objective of Office Kaizen. Wastes are the drivers of excess costs, delays, quality issues, and customer satisfaction shortfalls. *Surface wastes*, such as people not performing as well as they might under better circumstances (for example, better training, information, priority-setting, software, or sleep), are easily seen within organizations. The seemingly straightforward nature of surface waste creates a very large "blind spot" in general management practice. Managers mistakenly believe they are dealing with serious underlying issues when they address instances of surface waste. The critical problem for leadership is not one of knowing how to prevent a specific occurrence of waste. Instead, the critical problem is identifying the root cause of the waste and eliminating it. A patient who tells his doctor, "It hurts when I do this," and is told, "Don't do that anymore," has not been helped to eliminate the underlying problem.

The answer is to establish a system that attacks surface waste continually, without management itself having to point out each instance of waste or having to outline the solution. Without such a system, the same wastes keep appearing, despite having been "corrected" many times. Attacking surface wastes without a comprehensive philosophy is akin to trying to remove a wart by cutting off the top; it grows back from within.

PROCESS LEVELS AND MANAGEMENT STRATEGIES: THE LOGIC BEHIND OFFICE KAIZEN

Office Kaizen elevates the office and administrative portion of an organization's playing field above that of its competitors. This higher level of productivity, if sustained over time, provides a strategic competitive advantage. In order to explore why this is true, we must first discuss the optimum leverage points for improving competitive advantage at various organizational and process levels. Table 2.1 introduces the concept of micro-, macro-, and mega-processes.

Mega-processes operate at the senior executive level and encompass strategic planning, executive leadership, and market focus. Competitive

Table 2.1 Process levels, issues, and competitive leverage points.

Process Type	Characteristics	a. Example One b. Example Two	Common Leverage Points
Mega	Strategy, Executives, Markets, Strategic Relationships, Long-term planning	a. Should we acquire the XYZ company? b. Should we issue a credit card?	*Horizontal integration:* Buy or fight for market share? *Rationalizing:* Is this a business we should be in?
Macro	Tactics, Managers, Cross-functional integration, Products, Functions, Medium-term planning	a. Operate XYZ company separately or integrate it b. How do we provide customer service?	*Value-stream analysis:* Where is the money? *Make-buy analysis:* Who does it best?
Micro	Doing the day-to-day "work," Supervisors/workers, Processes, Office groups, Daily to weekly planning	a. How do we reduce order-processing costs? b. How do we reduce customer service cycle time?	*Process improvement:* How can we get it done better than any of our competitors

advantage at this level is dependent, to a large degree, on business rationalization; that is, deciding what businesses to be in. For a financial institution, a critical mega-process decision is whether or not to issue its own credit card. For service firms, a potential acquisition presents the mega-process dilemma of "fight for market share or buy it." An incorrect decision on either can be a deathblow in a highly competitive industry.

Operational executives and senior managers work at the macro-process level, where competitive advantage can be obtained through effective make–buy decisions and improvements to functional interfaces and value streams. For example, if a credit card is issued, bills must be generated and mailed—a process outsourced by most credit card issuers. Every business must decide to what extent it wishes to be vertically integrated. Once an acquisition decision is made, a necessary macro-process decision (with some mega-process issues, of course) involves whether or not to break up and integrate the acquisition or operate it completely (or somewhat) separately. A wrong decision at this level increases cycle time and costs and produces a competitive disadvantage.

The scale and duration of business success depends upon wise choices and execution at both the mega- and macro-process levels. This is why executives and senior managers are well compensated. Yet, no matter how wise the executive decision making and management execution may be, they are not enough for long-term success anymore. In any competitive market, it is very difficult for a market leader to develop a continuous stream of shocking new paradigms that provide a long-lasting competitive advantage at the mega- and macro-process levels. These days, everyone follows the innovative leader very rapidly and usually quite well.

Office Kaizen offers an exciting, new competitive advantage to be gained within the micro-process level. Market leaders in every administrative, engineering, and service industry have implemented, either through conscious planning or serendipity, at least some of the basics of Office Kaizen. They have significantly improved the performance of the hands-on workers and processes that produce their products and services. As long as these leaders do as well as the general industry at the mega- and macro-process levels, their outstanding performance at the micro-process level provides a long-lasting (and very difficult to copy) advantage. They use their micro-processes to lift themselves above an otherwise level playing field. One can buy technology and hire innovative leaders and managers, but micro-process improvements are realized the old-fashioned way— building them brick by brick at the work group level. Office Kaizen provides both the architectural drawings and the step-by-step construction plans to exploit this untapped competitive advantage.

One cannot create micro-process excellence with bold, new ideas or technology alone. In fact, micro-process problems are usually aggravated when additional technology is added by macro-level rescue efforts. A common example is providing a poorly performing project team with expensive and complex project management software. The result is almost always further schedule erosion, as people spend even more time at computers instead of dealing with each other face-to-face and resolving key issues.

Figure 2.1 demonstrates the key role of micro-process excellence in organizational success. Most organizations realize approximately the same benefits from bold, new macro- and mega-process ideas. The only differentiation, as shown in Figure 2.1, is the performance of the micro-processes upon which the bold, new ideas are placed. The left side of the figure displays the all too often seen situation in which a critically important initiative is brought to its knees by shoddy micro-process execution. How many implementations of enterprise information systems (EIS), the very symbol of modern business management technology, have been late and over budget due to hundreds of small, micro-process disconnects? The mega- and macro-process decisions are sound, but the execution of the day-to-day work at every level is compromised, often in ways that are beneath the radar of management. These shortfalls occur because there is no concerted effort to put in place a systematic approach for optimizing performance at the micro-process level. There is no Office Kaizen process improvement system in operation.

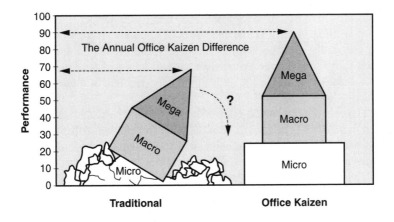

Figure 2.1 The key role of micro-processes in the success of all processes.

Office Kaizen focuses primarily on the improvement of micro-processes through the efforts of hands-on workers using what they already have—an extensive understanding of the processes they perform every day. Office Kaizen creates an organization characterized by the right side of Figure 2.1—macro- and mega-process, bold, new ideas that are allowed to reach their potential performance improvements, because the micro-process foundation is world class. In an Office Kaizen environment, this translates to:

- Optimization of existing processes with existing resources *before* new technology is added

- Extensive metrics and measurements kept by intact work groups

- Optimization of manual systems before automation is employed

- Extensive team involvement of intact work groups in setting micro-process goals and implementing action plans

- A foundation of excellence built around hundreds of small improvements

THE PARAMETERS OF LEADERSHIP AND THE OFFICE KAIZEN CUBE

What is the underlying cause of surface wastes? Most managers would answer that they are caused by too much or too little of one or more of the following: motivation, training, technology, communications, interpersonal skills, budgets, product design, software, supplier performance, education levels, technical skills, and so on. While these factors are relevant, they are rarely the true cause of surface waste. These commonly mentioned causes are created primarily by the presence of *leadership wastes,* or the wastes created within the leadership parameters of *focus, structure, discipline,* and *ownership.*

Figure 2.2 displays the Office Kaizen Cube. The Cube represents the basic logic of Office Kaizen. There is only one challenge that an enlightened leader must face: understanding and applying the Cube. Office Kaizen creates a structure that aggressively reduces leadership wastes (the top of the Cube) and enables standard and common tools to work to their full potential at all levels of the organization. If leadership wastes are sufficiently attenuated, surface wastes (the front of the Cube) will automatically decrease, no matter what tools, methods, or approaches are used. The tools are secondary to the elimination of leadership wastes. Costs, cycle time,

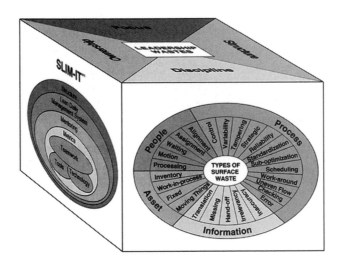

Figure 2.2   The Office Kaizen Cube.

customer satisfaction, and quality will all improve as surface wastes are reduced. The critical point illustrated by the Cube is that while long-term, constantly increasing, and sustainable surface waste reduction is the objective of Office Kaizen, it cannot be attained unless leadership waste is dramatically reduced at every level.

OFFICE KAIZEN AND SLIM-IT

The mechanism that powers Office Kaizen is SLIM-IT.* The left side of the cube shows the general elements of the SLIM-IT implementation model. SLIM-IT is the pronunciation of an acronym for Structure, Lean daily management system, Mentoring, Metrics, Tools, Teamwork and Technology. SLIM-IT, detailed in later chapters, is the mechanism that enables leadership to install and sustain Office Kaizen.

The individual techniques and methods of SLIM-IT have proven their ability to create tremendous competitive advantage for portions of many organizations over the last 30 years. Yet these achievements have only been a shadow of what can be attained. SLIM-IT takes the best of the "lessons

---

*SLIM-IT is a registered trademark of The Kaufman Consulting Group, LLC.

learned" and puts them together into one integrated, consistent package. It targets the leadership wastes of focus, structure, discipline, and ownership so that readily available tools (many of which are most likely already in place) can do what they were always supposed to do but could not: eliminate the surface waste that invisibly erodes initiatives and day-to-day productivity. SLIM-IT ensures that traditional, "here-today, gone-tomorrow" improvement efforts are replaced by the focus, structure, discipline, and ownership that encourage and sustain ongoing improvements. The result is Office Kaizen: the creation of an office and administrative culture that lifts that portion of an organization's playing field above the level at which its competitors continue to wallow.

3

Surface Wastes . . . The Silent Killers

George leaned back in his chair and suddenly realized that in an effort to stay ahead, he, as well as his leadership team, had been all over the board looking for quick fixes. They'd all participated in multiple "cutting the ribbon" ceremonies as they kicked off one initiative after another. Each event gave such promise, only to fizzle quickly once the real work was to begin. "Leadership parameters," mumbled George. "Due to lack of focus and leadership, we not only failed to reduce waste, we've spent a tremendous amount of time, money, and energy creating *more* waste." He felt his stomach churn. He kept reading.

Chapter 2 presented a high-level overview of Office Kaizen. Before delving into the mechanics of Office Kaizen in later chapters, it is important to clearly understand the significance of surface waste. At first glance, a serious consideration of surface waste almost seems beneath the dignity of an executive. The typical executive might think, "I've got more important things to worry about than the confusion over who authorizes special orders or needs to sign a form." The truth is that if an organization is fighting it out with more or less equally equipped competitors, an executive has few other concerns that merit as much attention as surface waste.

Consider a blood sample examined under an electron microscope. A virus is observed: a very small bit of quasi-life, less than one-millionth the volume of a single cell. One piece of the virus, however virulent, can do nothing if it simply circulates in the blood—even if it is the Ebola virus. But, if that small piece of virus gets into a cell and replicates, it will spread to every corner of the body. The virus need not be deadly to compromise the entire organism. A simple flu virus, if successful in replicating, can put a healthy person out of action for seven to 10 days.

This is exactly what waste is doing to organizations that are not practicing Office Kaizen right now; traditional organizations are infected at all levels by a surface waste flu. This virulent infection has been going on so long that it is often not recognized. As with our bodies, we either try to compensate for the weakness or ignore it, until a medical crisis finally shuts us down. Those few who are not so infected (award-winning industry leaders that stay in first place) are considered "lucky." Lucky, maybe, but most likely they have stumbled upon some of the secrets of Office Kaizen. They don't know it, but they have stumbled upon a vaccine that works for them. If we examine any of these vaccines, we would find that they contain many of the elements of Office Kaizen DNA.

Often, waste is obvious and visible to everyone. This is apparent whenever paperwork cannot be found or is incorrect. Waste can also appear suddenly, such as when a problem is not discovered until the customer finds it. Or perhaps an important payment is mishandled or a proposal doesn't get to the prospect on time. The waste is the cost of the lost business, damage control efforts, lost opportunities that could not be pursued because of the problem, and the diversion of management attention from the critical tasks of planning, leading, and relating to customers.

More often, waste is not visible or noticeable as it eats away at profits beneath the surface of everyday work. The requirement for an extra signature here, a delayed response to a phone inquiry there, two people doing the same work on different systems with different numbers, poorly run meetings, and project teams floundering without direction are all waste. Each of these wastes, and many, many more are voraciously devouring profits and alienating customers every day in every business. In all too many cases, the obvious surface wastes are accepted as "the way it is" or "part of the cost of doing business" or "people will be people." This is not the attitude that world-class organizations tolerate. They understand that waste is the number one killer of competitive success, and that Office Kaizen is the cure that can destroy it once and for all.

Office Kaizen operates much like hand washing and the sterilization of instruments works to reduce the probability of infection in operating rooms.

Joseph Lister, an English surgeon, was the first to sterilize instruments and wash his hands before operating. In an instant, infection and mortality rates for surgical cases (and everybody else the surgeons touched in the hospital) dropped "magically." Others rapidly adopted Lister's techniques, and the "magic" of aseptic operating theaters was born. These days, revolutionary MRI and laser techniques get most of the press as "magical" advances in surgery, but it is still critical that surgeons wash and that instruments be sterilized. In fact, experts from the Centers for Disease Control and Prevention still call hand washing the single most important way to stop infectious diseases from spreading. The lesson in all of this is that it makes no sense to pursue additional bold, new ideas if even more attention is not given to the elimination of the "simple" surface wastes that are killing profits a little bit every day.

Waste consists of resources consumed by activities that do not add value to a product or service. Whether an activity adds value or not must be determined from the perspective of the customer. That is, would a perfectly wise, all-knowing customer agree to pay for the activity if they had a choice? In other words, does the activity benefit the customer from their perspective? This hypothetical customer knows everything about what they want and how to optimize long-term costs, service quality, and performance successfully over the long term. While such an ideal customer does not exist, the perspective is essential. It provides a reference point from which a service or product producer can determine if an activity is value-added or waste.

For example, few customers would willingly agree to pay more for a bank loan in order to permit bank employees to use time and labor to locate documents that are misplaced. The customer views the searching as a waste of money. They desire an organization in which documents do not get lost in the first place, resulting in lower loan processing costs. Every organization has large amounts of this waste in its administrative and overhead budgets, and end-user customers are forced to pay for it. If a significant portion of this waste could be reduced, lower administrative costs would permit rate reductions and/or profit increases. Other instances of waste are more complex. Hard-working software engineers routinely over-endow software with needless complexities that few users want while not including features that most users need. No well-informed customer would willingly agree to pay for such foolishness if they had a choice. The organization that gives customers such a choice gets their business.

There are four categories of surface wastes that contain 26 specific types of waste. For each of these 26 classifications, a general description, a representative example, a traditional organization's short-term response, and the Office Kaizen solution are provided. As you review them, consider how many hundreds of times you have observed them (or their impacts) without really taking notice of them as silent killers.

PEOPLE WASTES

There are five *people wastes* that occur because organizations fail to harness the potential that resides in all work groups. Keep in mind that an instance of people waste does not carry with it any blame or attribution. Human beings have certain skills and behave in highly predictable ways. When people wastes occur, it is the fault of leadership for not properly structuring the work environment.

Goal Alignment Waste

Definition—Goal alignment waste is the energy expended by people working at cross-purposes and the effort required to correct the problem and produce a satisfactory outcome.

Example—An edict is issued to reduce travel expenses because sales have dropped off. The travel department implements policies that require all personnel to use tickets issued by the travel department at the lowest available ticket price. This forces sales people to take extra flight legs, leave home earlier, get home later, schedule fewer appointments in a week and so on. Complaints quickly follow, along with some resignations from highly skilled sales personnel who can easily find another job and be "treated better."

Typical Solution/Result—Sales, Human Resources, and Travel are told to "work together" and come up with an answer. After several months and many meetings, a thick volume of procedures is produced. Several sales people have already quit (along with a number of traveling technical personnel). Chances are, by the time the recommendations arrive, management has forgotten about it and the crisis has passed, because the business improved and the rules were changed (or Sales simply began to ignore the rules and do their own travel arrangements, thereby teaching everyone that policies are only recommendations). No customers would tolerate the built-in costs of such turnover, training of new hires, and wasted meetings.

The Office Kaizen Solution—In an Office Kaizen environment, the executive steering committee (ESC) charters a cross-functional change team to work out a solution that is cost-effective across the entire value stream over the long term. The team has a deadline for specific deliverables and the ESC reviews progress each week.

Assignment Waste

Definition—The effort used to complete an unnecessary or inappropriate task is assignment waste.

Example—A high-level manager tells a subordinate to prepare a report that details the process improvement department's training activities "in case the boss asks for it in the review meeting."

Typical Solution/Result—A glowing, "make everything look good" presentation is prepared that is most likely not used. If it is not used, the report preparation was a complete, one-time waste. If the report is used, the boss may like it, believe the deception, think that things are going well, and require all departments to submit such a report each month. The boss then spends time reviewing the reports and giving direction (requiring more lies and reports) instead of leading real, continuous improvement by implementing Office Kaizen. The waste is immense and horrific.

The Office Kaizen Solution—The Office Kaizen approach is to install the lean daily management system (LDMS) in each intact work group to ensure that small improvements are taking place. Also, the kaizen blitz change team reporting to the ESC constantly monitors sanctioned improvement activities. In addition, all ESC-chartered teams make brief reports to the ESC each week. This dramatically reduces the amount of improvement-related "fluff" reporting.

Waiting Waste

Definition—Waiting waste describes the resources lost as people wait for information, a meeting, a signature, a returned phone call, a copier or computer that is broken, and so on. People cannot add value to the product or service while they are waiting.

Example—Waiting on hold for a telephone call, a meeting to start, numbers, direction from a supervisor, and so on, are examples of waiting waste.

Typical Solution/Result—This is one of the common "accepted" wastes. If a high-level manager is annoyed by a specific instance, some training or coaching may be given but long-term change will not occur.

The Office Kaizen Solution—In an Office Kaizen environment, two avenues are used: 1) each intact work group uses the LDMS to monitor and improve its efficiency; over time, each intact work group begins to see that waiting is waste and will gradually reduce it; and 2) a change team reporting to the ESC conducts value stream mapping (or process flow) analyses that pinpoint the most blatant waiting wastes (differences between cycle time and total processing time). This permits additional change teams to address larger pockets of waiting that are caused by cross-functional issues.

Motion Waste

Definition—All movement that does not add value, such as walking and reaching, is waste.

Example—Inside sales personnel for a commodity product are required to leave their desks and walk to a FAX machine located at the far end of the room in order to send quotes. This means that they are often away from their desks when a customer calls. When the inside sales personnel return the calls, most of the time the potential customers have already placed their orders with someone else.

Typical Solution/Result—If the sales personnel complain, they are told to make fewer trips away from the phones (which forces the customers to wait longer to receive quotes).

The Office Kaizen Solution—Several avenues of improvement are possible: 1) with luck, the intact work group and/or its supervisor would understand that walking is waste (perhaps through introductory Office Kaizen training) and would construct a "spaghetti" diagram that details walking patterns in a typical day; follow-up brainstorming would then lead to suggestions to remove walking waste; or 2) a kaizen blitz team would do the same thing in a shorter time. Either of these approaches would then be supplemented by a "feet of walking required to process and order" metric that would be posted and periodically updated on the primary visual display board. The intact work group would continually strive to lower this metric.

Processing Waste

Definition—Any non-optimally performed work is processing waste. Employees are hard at work, but there is a better way to do the job.

Example—A pricing specialist is hard at work, never takes breaks and is always helpful and responsive. Yet he takes 20 percent longer to prepare each quote because he was not well trained.

Typical Solution/Result—Nothing would happen. Who would know? In the typical office, if there are no major mistakes and people appear to be busy, it is assumed that all is well, especially if the person has a good attitude. The crime here is that such a motivated person would be a highly productive, role-model employee who would feel less stress if the situation was addressed.

The Office Kaizen Solution—Each intact work group, led by the supervisor/ manager/lead, develops a set of best procedures that all members use. These procedures are used to provide training and certify that the worker has the necessary skills to do a job at a minimum level of performance. When improvements are discovered, they are incorporated into the "way work is done" so that all work group members benefit. Additionally, the posting of skill levels by job (on the primary visual display) assures that dedicated workers are recognized and that others are motivated to achieve similar recognition.

PROCESS WASTES

There are 12 *process wastes*. These wastes arise during the operation of business processes as a result of process design and execution shortfalls. There is a great deal of interaction between all categories of waste, and many processing wastes could be discussed as "people" wastes, but this would serve to camouflage the detailed etiology of specific waste occurrences.

Control Waste

Definition—Control waste is energy used for supervision or monitoring that does not produce sustainable, long-term improvements in overall performance. A large part of traditional supervision and management interaction with employees is control waste.

Example—A purchasing manager "walks the floor" through their department several times a day to "see who is doing what." It is assumed that people are doing their jobs if they are at their desks or are "looking busy."

Typical Solution/Result—If someone is away from their desk and talking with other employees, the manager calls the employee into the office and provides counseling. If there is an intervening supervisor, the manager speaks to the supervisor who then speaks with the employee in separate counseling sessions. This results in extra down time on the part of everyone and compromises the opportunity to refocus an employee's commitment. Also, a great deal of such "counseling" is counterproductive: it demeans and insults many good workers who are attempting to fix real problems.

The Office Kaizen Solution—The LDMS focuses intact work groups on key processes and metrics. Problems quickly surface when metrics do not improve as they should. Improvement suggestions are captured by the kaizen action sheet system within each intact work group. Instead of patrolling and reacting to appearances, management's role becomes one of coaching the maintenance of the LDMS and its components.

Variability Waste

Definition—Resources expended to compensate for and/or correct outcomes that deviate from expected or typical outcomes create variability waste.

Example—A customer expects, based upon prior experience, to receive a reimbursement check from his insurance company within four weeks of filing a claim. When the check does not arrive in week four, the customer calls the claims department. The claims department must research the claim and call the customer back. Over the next week, the customer calls several more times, initiating additional searches by personnel not familiar with the earlier calls, because two of them are new employees and/or they do not fully understand the customer service data input system. Dozens of calls are made. The check was mailed only one week late due to a number of small, routine delays in the system. The customer receives the check before the claims department calls the customer to tell him that the check will arrive soon.

Typical Solution/Result—If the problem is not surfaced to a higher level, nothing is done. If it gets attention, the common response is to initiate more controls and checks. These only add more delays and reports and slow down the overall system even more. The customer screams in agony while he waits for a check.

The Office Kaizen Solution—One or both of two improvement avenues would operate: 1) the LDMS would gradually improve elements of the process value chain within each intact work group that is involved; or 2) if the improvements don't amount to enough (or are not realized fast enough), a kaizen blitz or a change team reporting to the ESC would augment the efforts by conducting value stream mapping or related analyses.

Tampering Waste

Definition—The effort used to arbitrarily change a process without understanding all of the consequences, and the effort required to compensate for or correct the unexpected consequences of the arbitrary change, are tampering wastes.

Example—A manager, upset over an incorrectly submitted bit of paperwork that delays a critical customer order, issues a procedure that requires his review and sign-off of each order.

Typical Solution/Result—All orders are delayed, some as much as three to five days when the manager is traveling. When a manager from another department is given "signing" authority, he doesn't know what to look for and more mistakes are sent to customers. The resulting loss of business is attributed by the manager to the customers' ire at the original isolated delays, not his deceleration of the entire system.

The Office Kaizen Solution—In an Office Kaizen environment, a significant performance issue would result in the addition of key tracking metrics that the intact work group would place on its primary visual display and review daily at the work group meeting.

Strategic Waste

Definition—Strategic waste is value lost (effort wasted) as a result of employing processes that satisfy short-term goals and/or internal customer needs but do not provide value to customers and shareholders.

Example—A new software system is installed to cut down on a number of information wastes (to be discussed below). The decision itself is wise, but the manner in which it is carried out is not. The company decides to buy an "off-the-shelf" software system and performs extensive customization to make it comply with the idiosyncrasies of the company's processes. The better course is to buy the best software needed and change the company's processes so that minimal, or ideally no, customization is required.

Typical Solution/Result—The result is massive delays, huge overruns in programming costs, more complicated procedures, more errors, and horrendous costs in the future in order to customize as upgrades occur. The objective (a new system) was wise; the strategy for attaining it created massive waste.

The Office Kaizen Solution—The ESC would charter a team or teams to assess needs over the entire business value chain impacted by the software. Then this team, or several, guides the selection and implementation of the software. The decision to go "custom" versus "off-the-shelf" is still a leadership decision but Office Kaizen provides a more solid foundation for the decision.

Reliability Waste

Definition—Reliability waste is effort required for correction of unpredictable process outcomes due to initially unknown causes.

Example—Jack and Madison have been working together as a team for several years in the proposal department. Over time, their responsibilities evolved into a dependable routine, each handling certain aspects of each proposal, almost on automatic pilot. However, due to increased business, two new people, both hard workers and skilled, join the department. A month later, Madison takes a long-planned vacation. Nobody catches the absence of an overhead adjustment factor on a price quote in a large, complex proposal. This had always been Madison's task, so Jack does not think about it; the two new people do not know to look for it. The incredibly low-priced quote wins the business, and the company, forced to honor it, loses over two hundred thousand dollars.

Typical Solution/Result—More controls and signatures are required in the future. Madison and Jack feel oppressed and insulted by the additional controls and transfer to other jobs or leave the company. The new people, being less experienced, take 20 percent longer to do proposals, and the company loses additional business. This waste is due to the lack of a checklist or responsibility/authority task matrix (a standard reengineering and Office Kaizen tool).

The Office Kaizen Solution—One or all of three mutually supportive techniques would be applied: 1) the intact work group (Jack and Madison) would develop a standard work process that is graphically displayed and periodically reviewed for improvements; 2) a cross-training matrix for the intact work group (and perhaps across nearby process groups as well) would be developed so that no person would be asked to do a job unless he or she had been trained to a sufficient level. Each task would have a group-developed (and management approved) procedure that, over time, teaches many workers to do many tasks skillfully; and 3) the intact work group would continually develop additional check sheets and job aids that would be folded into the standard work process and the training materials.

Standardization Waste

Definition—Energy wasted because a job isn't done the best way by all those who do it.

Example—Monica runs a customer service call center that takes orders and manages delivery and service issues. All of her people work very hard, but some do better than others. Although Evan is not the most experienced employee in the group, he routinely processes more calls and makes fewer mistakes than the other workers. In his two years on the job, he has developed an impressive array of checklists and other job aids that help him avoid errors and provide better service.

Typical Solution/Result—If Monica is a typical manager, she exalts Evan as an "ideal" employee and encourages others to do as well. She may try contests or incentives to improve the others' performance. Although a burst of improvement may be realized, poor or inefficient habits inevitably return.

The Office Kaizen Solution—The entire intact work group uses Evan's job aids because they are incorporated into the skills versatility training. The result is that everyone uses the best approaches possible.

Suboptimization Waste

Definition—Processes competing with one another cause suboptimization waste. In the best case, the only waste is the duplicated work. In the worst case, competing processes compromise each other and degrade the final outcome.

Example—Acme Corporation has many locations. The purchasing departments in all of the locations are attempting to reduce the total number of suppliers and establish more "partner-like" relationships with the remaining suppliers. It is Acme's hope that this will reduce purchasing administration costs and suppliers' prices while providing higher quality. At the same time, the product development managers of each site negotiate on their own with a select group of specialty suppliers to obtain absolutely the lowest possible prices on parts/services for each new development effort. The designers do this so they can claim a lower total product cost for their prototype (this cost is a large factor in their performance reviews). A prototype parts supplier who provides the lowest price cannot afford to participate very much in design efforts; critical supplier input is missed in the development of all new prototypes, thereby compromising the final product. When prototype development is followed by a production run, it is difficult for the "partnered" volume suppliers to compete with the prototype supplier. They provide a lot of technical assistance but cannot be as low cost as the prototype supplier. As a result, the prototype suppliers win the business, or a partnered supplier gets the contract by matching the prototype supplier's price but cannot afford to include any "partnering" activities and support. Poor products are designed and the entire partnering effort ends up meaning nothing. Everybody loses.

Typical Solution/Result—The typical result is to blame the suppliers for the problems instead of requiring Development and Purchasing to work together from the start to establish the lowest lifecycle costs.

The Office Kaizen Solution—Two methods would be employed: 1) at the corporate level, a chartered, cross-functional team would develop corporate purchasing agreements for all locations that covered key commodity and off-the-shelf materials; and 2) at each site, a cross-functional change team reporting to the ESC would be formed and tasked to develop procedures that compel the materials, purchasing, and design engineering personnel to work together to attain the best overall costs.

Scheduling Waste

Definition—Resources wasted by compensating for poorly scheduled activities are scheduling waste.

Example—There are 10 administrative assistants supporting the 10 executive officers of Megatechservices, Inc. Each works more or less independently, although they help each other when required to cover phones or assist with big projects. Some of them have very heavy, steady workloads while others have wildly fluctuating workloads. A few, with computer-savvy bosses, have light workloads. Occasionally, around quarterly report time, several of the assistants discover they cannot finish the massive workload on time. They ask their colleagues for help, but assistance comes in 30- to 60-minute increments due to the volunteers being pulled away by their bosses.

Typical Solution/Result—The organization hires temporary staff or has lower-level managers "volunteer" to loan their administrative personnel to help for a day or two. Because the temporary helpers are not familiar with the details, the result is poor quality and a lot of rework.

The Office Kaizen Solution—The administrative assistants form an intact work group and work as a team to support all of the executives. This work group installs an LDMS and works to continually improve work balance and reaction time to demands.

Work-Around Waste

Definition—Work-around waste occurs when resources are used to create and maintain informal processes that replace "official" processes or conflict with other informal processes, as well as the resources used to correct errors caused by using such systems.

Example—Many people at Nine Lives Benefit Plans, Ltd. generate quotes for group coverage. The company has a formal quoting system, but it is not user-friendly. Several years ago, an enterprising employee developed a spreadsheet program that duplicated the formal system but was less complex if the user made some manual inputs from paper sources. Over the years, different employees and managers modified the spreadsheet to suit their needs and distributed it among colleagues. Several attempts to stamp out the spreadsheet programs were made over the years by various managers (when large errors in pricing slipped through), but the spreadsheets are still used secretly (and are continually updated) by most employees.

Typical Solution/Result—A massive crackdown with penalties and more control would be the most typical traditional response. Such tactics never work for long and low morale and frustration prevail until the next crackdown occurs.

The Office Kaizen Solution—The ESC would charter a team of cross-functional users and software support people. The change team would then develop a single method that would have the benefits of the best of the spreadsheet programs with the reliability of the company system.

Uneven Flow Waste

Definition—Resources invested in material or information that piles up between workstations create uneven flow waste.

Example—The marketing department of Mega Industries is hiring new sales representatives. Human Resources, having been told that it is critical to staff up as soon as possible, schedules the candidates for interviews with hiring managers. As a result, seven candidates appear one Monday morning, two days before the quarterly sales conference. Interviews are chaotic, interrupted by phone calls and visits from staffers (review this, look at that, and so on), abbreviated, and sometimes passed on to managers in other departments. Many candidates are unimpressed with the disorder, and several less than stellar candidates are hired, because they received great reviews from noninvolved managers.

Typical Solution/Result—Human Resources castigates the hiring departments, who blame Human Resources, and nothing much of lasting impact happens.

The Office Kaizen Solution—The ESC of the site charters a change team to plan and manage all aspects of the anticipated surge in employment, from recruiting to on-boarding.

Checking Waste

Definition—Effort used for inspection (and rework) is checking waste.

Example—In a law office, briefs and motions are sent out with many typographical errors (as a result of many new employees). Most are minor, but several create embarrassment for the firm.

Typical Solution/Result—The traditional response is to double and triple proofreading, often by a highly paid (compared to support staff) paralegal or intern. In a more Draconian environment, an escalating series of reprimands and discipline might be instituted to "motivate" correct transcription. The waste of checking is significant, some errors still get through and turnover increases even more.

The Office Kaizen Solution—The word processors or administrative assistants are formed into intact work teams. These teams institute appropriate successive check procedures within each intact work group. These are reviewed at daily work group meetings and revised as necessary. If this is not sufficient, the law firm's ESC charters a change team to address the issue.

Error Waste

Definition—Error waste refers to resources required to duplicate work that is rendered useless by an error.

Example—We all know thousands of them.

Typical Solution/Result—In most environments, it is assumed that a certain number of errors is inevitable. When the number gets too big (or the impact of a single error is extreme), the response is usually more checking, disciplinary threats, and/or additional procedures. Errors decrease for a while but always come back when the crisis passes and attention lags.

The Office Kaizen Solution—Each intact work group tracks all errors daily and reviews them once a day at its work group meeting. The group (led by the supervisor) then takes corrective action by adding successive checks, changes in processes (error proofing), and/or installing job aids. If these methods are not sufficient, the ESC charters a change team to provide additional analysis and support.

INFORMATION WASTE

Information waste is a subset of process waste but one so important that it must be called out on its own. It is the loss of value caused by less than optimum information. There are five types.

Translation Waste

Definition—Translation waste is effort required to change data, formats, and reports between process steps or owners. Translation waste can be extreme in organizations, consuming the time of managers, analysts, and administrative personnel. Worse, it leads to costly mistakes.

Example—The most recent, well-known instance of translation waste involved the Mars Polar Lander fiasco. A missed translation of English to metric units destroyed a $170 million U.S. spacecraft.

Typical Solution/Result—The most common instances of translation waste go unnoticed, as process steps move from spreadsheets to mainframe systems to manual operations. When translation waste causes a big problem, the response is more checking and procedures, flavored with a bit of disciplinary action. The waste of accompanying "blame assignment" is always massive if the error is large or visible. Translation waste in the form of report "packaging" (award-winning PowerPoint presentations) is encouraged in a great many organizations and often rewarded by executive management.

The Office Kaizen Solution—The only solution to translation waste is strong leadership that focuses on results and real data rather than "flash." Office Kaizen helps open executives' eyes to the waste of useless reporting, but they will have to be strong to buck the societal trend that glorifies presentation expertise and excuses over applied results. The Office Kaizen approach to such an important mission as the Mars Polar Lander would be for the project ESC to charter a team (or teams) to metric map (and value stream map) every detail of processes so that there were no loose, unknown ends.

Missing Information Waste

Definition—Missing information waste refers to resources required to repair the consequences of or compensate for the absence of key information.

Example—A salesperson for Acme Widgets puts an order into the system without complete information so that it "can get a jump start." She intends to provide the remaining data as soon as she can check with the warehouse, but she forgets to make the call. The order is processed incorrectly, shipped, and then returned by the angry customer.

Typical Solution/Result—The salesperson is told to "try harder next time." If the consequences are severe, either the salesperson or someone in Shipping is blamed and additional audits are put in place.

The Office Kaizen Solution—The ESC charters a team that includes sales and order processing personnel to reengineer the entire process so that faster processing can be achieved without compromising accuracy. Additionally, key metrics to assure compliance are collected daily and reviewed on the primary visual displays of the appropriate intact work groups.

Hand-Off Waste

Definition—Hand-off waste is the effort required to transfer information (or materials) within an organization (departments and groups) that are not fully integrated into the process chain being used.

Example—The operations department of a mergers and acquisitions company plans for new facilities and office space on a yearly basis. They forward their information to the planning department. The planning department "adjusts" the numbers to incorporate nominal yield calculations, amortization on previous years' expenditures, and so on. The information is then passed back to Operations. Much time is lost, unnecessary changes are incorporated, and each function feels that it is being manipulated by the other.

Typical Solution/Result—A few meetings and discussions occur that exhort everyone to work together better, but nothing changes.

The Office Kaizen Solution—The ESC appoints a change team to develop a system that does a better job faster. Involved intact work groups track key metrics daily on their primary visual displays.

Irrelevancy Waste

Definition—Effort employed to deal with unnecessary information, or the effort required to fix problems that it causes, is irrelevancy waste.

Example—Bet Your Life Insurance, Inc. institutes a continuous improvement system. In a well-intentioned effort to motivate managers to support continuous improvement activities, a process improvement weekly report is required from each supervisor and manager. It requires data on the number of teams working on problems (and their activities), the number of suggestions submitted and acted upon, and the resulting dollar savings achieved.

Typical Solution/Result—In a desperate effort to achieve good-looking numbers, managers and supervisors push for any and all suggestions, valid or not, and form teams to address every conceivable issue. Financial benefits are shamelessly inflated and the entire continuous improvement effort suffers from the sham. Thousands of hours are wasted in preparing and polishing reports that are worse than worthless; they teach employees and managers to be cynical and distrusting of management and its actions.

The Office Kaizen Solution—The LDMS with its kaizen action sheet system is installed into each intact work group. This approach permits each work group to manage its own small improvements. The ESC charters only necessary teams to work on issues that it approves. The role of management in "achieving improvements" becomes one of maintaining the LDMS–ESC structure, not one of motivating and reviewing worthless dreck.

Inaccuracy Waste

Definition—Inaccuracy waste is effort used to create incorrect information or deal with the consequences of it.

Example—After-hours phone service representatives make errors when updating changes in the next day's appointments for service representatives. In about five percent of the cases, they enter the wrong date or hour (or both). Much service time is wasted and many customers get upset.

Typical Solution/Result—The most typical response is disciplinary action against those who make the errors. If the errors continue, systems changes might be suggested to put more of the burden on the software to prevent errors. This is expensive and takes a long time.

The Office Kaizen Solution—Each intact work group tracks all errors daily and reviews them once a day at its work group meeting. The group (led by the supervisor) then takes appropriate corrective action. If this is not sufficient, the ESC charters a change team to address larger cross-functional issues or those that might require complex software changes.

ASSET WASTE

Asset waste is created by the less than optimal utilization of material and property. When a building, office supplies, parts, products, and service delivery materials are not used in the most efficient manner to add value, asset waste occurs. There are four asset wastes.

Inventory Waste

Definition—All process resources that are applied to a service before they are required, all raw material that is not being used, and all material that is ready to be shipped but is being held are inventory wastes.

Example—A marketing services firm has a slow day. Several of the employees are put to work stuffing 10,000 advertising brochures that will be sent out over the next month. Two weeks later, a typo is discovered on one of the inserts and all of the as yet unsent brochures must be taken apart.

Typical Solution/Result—A great deal of attention is paid to the cause of the typo.

The Office Kaizen Solution—Intact work groups track their productivity (via metrics on their primary visual display boards). They have contingency plans to put unexpected idle time to productive use (training, workplace organization, error-proofing, and so on) rather than just keeping busy. When a large project is approaching (such as a need to send out 10,000 brochures in two weeks), intact work groups are notified and they work in advance to plan how to support each other without doing the work in advance.

Work-in-Process Waste

Definition—Resources expended in mid-process that cannot yet be used by downstream process steps are work-in-process wastes.

Example—An insurance company has 30 people in one of its medical claims processing departments. They all work in very narrow job classifications. The bottleneck part of the process is mid-stream, where two employees place diagnosis and treatment codes into each file. Typically, there are 300 to 700 claim forms waiting in queue for them to process. The workers downstream are often "out of work," because they can easily keep up with the bottleneck.

Typical Solution/Result—Managers do not like to see idle workers, so they either send the waiting workers to help in the upstream processes or tell them to help the coders. The first tactic generates even more of a pile in front of the two coders. The second tactic creates more errors.

The Office Kaizen Solution—Four simultaneous approaches are applied: 1) the claims department is broken up into a number of intact work groups. First within intact work groups and then between them, workers are cross-trained so they can move between jobs and maintain high skill levels; 2) the entire process is reengineered to streamline the work flow; 3) an 80–20 analysis (what 20 percent of the tasks take 80 percent of the time and what tasks require lower skill levels?) is done on the critical bottleneck tasks, and a small group of workers is formed into a work cell to handle coding; and 4) the backlog at each station is monitored daily on each intact work group's primary visual display. This provides advance warning and reaction time for developing problems.

Fixed Asset Waste

Definition—Resources tied up in equipment and buildings that are not maximally used are called fixed asset wastes.

Example—Under Your Mattress Banking Corporation leases five floors of a large building. The company needs more space for new employees necessitated by growth. No attempt is made to determine if existing space could be better utilized before more space is added.

Typical Solution/Result—The typical response is to lease more space.

The Office Kaizen Solution—First, the ESC forms a team to help each work area reduce its floor space and develop an overall plan. Second, each intact work group uses layout tools and workplace organization methods to remove unnecessary storage and space.

Moving Things Waste

Definition—All transport of materials and information, except that used to deliver products and services directly to customers, is waste.

Example—An organization is based on a campus with many buildings. Over the years, departments and sections have made many moves to accommodate growth and changes in the services they offer. There is much walking back and forth between buildings to go to meetings, obtain signatures, meet with customer and supplier representatives, and look at documentation. High-status groups are always lobbying for choice, in-the-middle-of-campus locations and everyone else is always complaining.

Typical Solution/Result—Management encourages everyone to use more e-mail and teleconferences when possible. This results in less face-to-face time, less cross-functional cooperation (resulting in more suboptimization) and even more movement waste as people are required to attend "emergency" fix-it meetings.

The Office Kaizen Solution—The ESC charters a team (or teams) to prioritize major processes that involve substantial movement around the campus. Each highly ranked process is then reengineered to reduce walking. This is done by the creation of co-located offices, group conference facilities, and the like.

DEALING WITH SURFACE WASTE

Any one instance of surface waste is not difficult to deal with if one knows what to look for, recognizes what is seen, and has the time and resources to take action. The problem is that management (at all levels) is consciously aware of only one to two percent of everyday waste occurrences. Most waste operates unseen or is even encouraged by mistaken approaches for dealing with people and processes. This is one of the reasons why almost any kaizen blitz or reengineering effort unearths surprising, vast amounts of improvement opportunity even in "well-run organizations." Once the filters of traditional waste tolerance/blindness are removed from management's (and employees') eyes, hundreds of instances of waste appear and can be addressed. Even after more than 20 years of directing reengineering and blitz efforts in countless environments, I am always shocked (shocked!) at how much more waste is uncovered by even the most limited investigation—even in well-run organizations. It is everywhere. It *is* traditional business.

However, recognizing instances of waste and implementing corrective measures is not enough to create lasting improvements, much less a world-class office environment. After all, thousands upon thousands of organizations have employed reengineering and blitzes and discovered their hidden oceans of waste. Why aren't there more world-class office environments? The answer is that few organizations have been able to dramatically improve their performance, much less become world class, through reengineering and kaizen blitzes alone.

Consider the three statements below:

a. A process is "fixed" and waste is reduced

b. A process is "fixed" and remains "fixed" over time, even after the excitement and attention (resources, fun, sense of urgency) of the reengineering effort is over

c. The process is "fixed" and steady reductions of the same waste are achieved over time without special reengineering efforts or management intervention

Anyone with four hours of training can do "a" in almost any situation or environment. Only one environment in 20 can do "b" without special intervention from management. It is not uncommon to find that changes created by outstanding reengineering/kaizen blitz efforts completely disappear in six months. Only one organization in 1000 (to be charitable) can do "c": reengineer a process, have it maintained by those who use it, *and* have those who use it continue to make small improvements in it. Creating sustainable, focused, disciplined change has always been the challenge for leaders. As demonstrated in the remaining chapters of this book, Office Kaizen meets this challenge "head on."

4

Leadership Waste and the Executive Challenge

George was excited and anxious. He could relate to the prevalence and impact of surface wastes with every molecule of his body and with every entry on his resume. He had witnessed the same thing in every place he'd worked and he had always resented it. "I've spent half my business life dealing with the consequences of such waste," he thought, "and they keep happening!" Although George believed himself to be at least a part-time visionary, he hadn't even thought about creating a strategic advantage through the reduction of surface wastes. While aggravated by the wastes, he thought organizations had to live with them. "How much might be gained if wastes could be reduced a small but significant amount across the board, in every office and on every desk? Yes, Office Kaizen could be a strategic competitive weapon," he thought, "if it works."

The previous chapter established the importance of reducing surface waste to generate a unique, sustainable competitive advantage. Hopefully this information created an appreciation of the insidious central position of surface waste in degrading competitiveness. Now, let's move far upstream to the most important target of Office Kaizen: *leadership waste*.

The entire structure of Office Kaizen rests upon the absolute, critical need to reduce leadership waste at all levels of the organization. Titanic, natural, and omnipresent forces can confound the best-led efforts if leadership wastes are not reduced in a systematic manner. As stated in chapter 3, if leadership wastes could be dramatically reduced by "magic" in an organization, it wouldn't matter what additional tools and approaches were applied; the organization would be incredibly successful. However, the reduction of leadership waste requires a methodology to remove enough leadership waste so that surface waste reduction tools can be effective. Office Kaizen is that methodology. Any approach that reduces surface waste in an organization and continues to reduce it over an extended period is benefiting from some of the leadership waste reduction benefits of Office Kaizen (no matter what it's called). If the goal is continuous, long-term reduction of surface waste, it must always start with the reduction of leadership wastes. Otherwise, surface waste tools cannot do their jobs properly.

As you will see in chapter 5, the normal resting state of organizations acts to decrease the four leadership parameters of focus, structure, discipline, and ownership. In a carefully led environment, these parameters will naturally increase and provide the substance for a world-class organization. Given this reality, the thrust of Office Kaizen is the creation of an environment where the reduction of leadership waste is always underway.

FOCUS

Focus is the application of energy and attention to critical objectives. Focus must be present at every level of the organization in an appropriate manner. When a CEO affirms that their company will "expand into Europe," "provide better customer service," "become a preferred supplier," and/or "dominate the industry through low costs," they are attempting to provide some focus. Just stating the focus at the executive level is the easy part. The real challenge is driving the focus down into the organization and maintaining its accuracy at every level. Almost every organization has had an executive-level push for "improved quality" at some point. Yet, despite extensive management attention to the issue, it is common to find that various portions and levels of an organization pursue "improved quality" with immensely wide-ranging varieties of interest, accuracy, and effect. I experienced this firsthand when I was employed at one of the "Big Three" U.S. automakers. The CEO released a quality improvement mandate. Our plant held huge "all hands" meetings in which quality was discussed, competitors' performance was contrasted with the plant's performance, and the plant manager and visiting dignitaries gave rousing speeches.

One department responded by developing and installing a comprehensive series of timely metrics in each supervisor section and then briefing each group three times per week. This was a very good first step. Another department installed a system for tracking errors and gave workers individual feedback, along with an escalating series of disciplinary actions for repeat errors. This was a very bad move as the workers then hid problems to protect each other (and many errors had nothing to do with employees' actions, such as paint defects caused by air pressure problems). Other groups did nothing. They reacted to the quality initiative in the same way as they had to all of the prior "programs" that had arrived at a rate of two to three per year—nod the head, agree, do nothing, and wait for a few months until it passes.

The CEO had stated the focus clearly. However, the message was understood differently as it filtered down through the organization. Somewhere between the CEO and the work groups, the focus was distorted, misdirected, or just plain stopped. Every worker and work group must get the same message in a manner that they understand and that applies to them in the job they do each day.

Think of the CEO's focus as a bright beam of light shining into the organization from above. The objective is to have the enlightened focus of the CEO's beam illuminate the true path to success for members of the organization that are struggling in the darkness of traditional management. Some employees can perceive only red light, others see only ultraviolet, and some can detect only green. Some, of course, have been blinded by years of darkness. Another problem is that many employees are obstructed from receiving the CEO's beam continuously, if at all. The barriers of processes, departments, work groups, shifts, geographical locations, different products, different supervisory practices, and varying customer demands serve to block, distort, refract, bend, minimize, or amplify the CEO's beam. Finally, some employees and employee groups don't pay attention to the light when it shines. They have not seen a difference for themselves or their work groups whether it is dark or light in their work area.

Focus is supplied by making sure the message from the CEO (or other senior executives/managers) gets to everyone in a manner they can understand. Without focus, there is no possibility for the entire organization to move together in a coordinated manner; too much energy will be lost to internal friction. Each employee must understand what is important to the organization in terms that relate to his or her job.

While all four of the leadership parameters are necessary and essential to success in any situation in which changes must be made, focus is the most important. You can have the best gun and ammunition in the world, but if you can't aim accurately (see the target; hold your body, shoulder, arm, and hand steady), you will miss. At the same time, focus is often the hardest of the leadership parameters to establish, because it seems the least concrete. The mechanisms of Office Kaizen are designed to help in this regard. Even before an organization's overall focus is explicitly understood, the techniques of Office Kaizen implicitly help develop and nurture portions of it within all work groups. This is because the reduction of leadership waste and surface waste is a universal condition for improvement in every work group no matter what the work or the content of leadership's objectives. That is, less waste always helps the bigger picture. Office Kaizen begins to get all employees focused on eliminating waste, regardless of the overall mission of the organization.

FOCUS WASTE

It is easy to get a rough idea of how much *focus waste* is present in an organization. Ask yourself how you or your employees would respond to the following true/false statements:

1. I can state the principle objectives of the overall organization for the current year.

2. I was told in person how the overall organization performed on its principle objectives last year.

3. I know the primary objectives that my work group must attain during the current year to meet its plan.

4. The primary objectives of my work group for the current year were fully explained to the entire group.

5. I have a clear picture of how the overall organization compares to its competitors in terms of costs, delivery, quality, and customer satisfaction.

6. I understand how my work group compares to similar work groups at competitor organizations in terms of costs, delivery, quality, customer satisfaction, and status vis-à-vis world-class performance.

7. I understand what drives price, cost, and competitiveness in our industry.

8. My work group's critical objectives for the current year are defined with easy-to-understand, objective measures.

9. Everyone in my work group understands exactly how we compare to world-class work groups that do similar tasks.

10. My work group receives detailed updates (at least weekly) from our supervisor or leader about how we are doing.

An instance of focus leadership waste occurs each time an individual employee answers "false" to one of the above statements. These thousands of little instances of focus waste every month eat away at correct priority setting, willingness to make sacrifices, resolve to fight for improvements, and the accuracy of subjective decision making when no clear guidelines are available. Each instance of such waste creates untold opportunities for surface waste to occur.

STRUCTURE

Structure is the skeleton of an organization. Every organization has a structure, even if management and employees cannot explicitly describe it. Many equate structure with organization charts, titles, department names, and process flowcharts, but structure is much, much more. Just as good soup is more than the ingredients that float on the surface, an organization's structure consists of the processes, expectations, rituals and behaviors, roles (expected, enacted, and ideal, as well as their conflicts, both within and between people), and information. Structure is the written and unwritten rules, guidelines, processes, and behaviors that are actually followed, not simply stated. In a sentence, structure is the repeatable, generally constant framework that guides what happens day-to-day in an organization.

Most organizations' structures have evolved haphazardly over time. Organizational charts may be constructed with considerable attention to detail, but little else is done with careful planning. The unspoken rules in most organizations are usually an interactive product of many years of random influences, responses to crises, human group dynamics, and leadership initiatives. This results in not one, but many, structures in most organizations.

Major banks are good examples of organizations with multiple structures. There may be a single corporate structure that influences some activities to a degree over all of the organization's locations across several states. This corporate structure will be minimal if the bank was recently formed from many mergers and acquisitions (which is probably the case with most very large banks today). There most certainly will be a structure in each bank's regional headquarters office (especially since each of these offices was probably an independent bank headquarters only a few years ago).

Further, each of the departments, branches, and processing centers (and their departments) within regions will have varying structures.

Some elements of these structures are forced by industry standards (for example, rules for balancing books, accounting standards, laws about when banks may be closed). Some portions of the structure are determined by the types of people that work in various technologies and skills. There will be vastly different structures for those who work in the data processing center, frontline tellers, and the corporate law department. Each has its own functionally influenced set of expectations, roles, freedoms, dress codes, and reporting formalities.

The analogy of the CEO shining their beam of focus into the organization can be extended to include the structure leadership parameter. The structure is the functioning set of mirrors, prisms, filters, and amplifiers and the framework to hold them in place. It also includes the specifications as to what sort of light (color and brightness) each work group requires, as well as instructions for building the entire device throughout the organization (location and angle of each light-guiding device, as well as the pieces of the supporting framework). Properly designed and built, the structure directs the correct type of light to all parts of the organization. World-class organizations have developed structures that direct leadership's focus more accurately and reliably to every work group than the average organization.

Of course, there is more to structure than simply directing focus. That is hard enough, but the structure must also provide guidance and direction as to what employees should do and how they should do it in ways that reduce surface wastes, keep them reduced, and eliminate more of them in the future.

STRUCTURE WASTE

Structure waste occurs when existing behaviors, expectations, procedures, rituals, regulations, roles, and priorities do not reinforce, guide, and coach optimum behaviors for reducing surface waste. Office Kaizen addresses the structure waste created by the differences between an organization's existing structure and the universal elements found in world-class organizations; and the differences between the conflicting structures found in separate portions of an organization. Think about how you or your employees might respond to the following true or false statements to determine the extent to which structure waste may be present in your organization:

1. My everyday processes and tasks are well defined.

2. I track my personal performance on a daily basis with numerical measures.

3. Most of my work group's processes are clearly defined and understood by most group members.

4. Managers make it easy to understand their decisions.

5. My work group's supervisor (manager, lead person, and so on) provides us with timely information about changes so that we can respond quickly.

6. My work group is supervised much the same as other work groups in the organization in terms of supervisory attitudes, help, friendliness, and the amount of information we have about our jobs.

7. My work group has a short (five to 10 minutes) daily meeting to bring us up to date on what is happening today and how we did yesterday.

8. For many problems that occur in my work group, there is a single course of action that almost everybody in the work group understands.

9. My work group's supervisor (manager, lead person, and so on) actively assists me in learning more about my tasks and those of other work group members.

10. My work group has a formal plan to gradually improve the performance of day-to-day processes over the next couple of years.

An organization without world-class structures in each work group is much like the muscles of a world-class body builder without a skeleton; however well developed, it will just flop around. The best employees in the world, even with great focus, must have a means of exerting leverage on their day-to-day work. In a human body, bones do this. In an organization, the roles, behaviors, and expectations provide the leverage points for the people to hold onto as they strain against surface wastes.

DISCIPLINE

Without discipline, focus and structure are merely necessary but insufficient elements for successful leadership. They are of little use if the organization cannot maintain them over time (much like being on a well-designed and medically proven diet with great diet books and all sorts of diet food in the freezer, but then cheating). *Discipline* consists of the checks and balances, rewards, compulsions, and daily behaviors (by management and employees) that maintain the processes of leadership. That is, people do what they are expected to do, and, if they don't, somebody or some group finds out quickly and gets them back on track.

In our light analogy, the discipline involves checking to assure that the light source is powered and operating properly, monitoring the mirrors to assure that they are correctly angled and clean, and examining the framework holding the mirrors to assure that it is not rusting and/or out of alignment. The best light source and the best initial mirror system installation are of little use if they are allowed to drift off target over time. Then, of course, there is the even bigger issue of what the employees do once they have the benefit of the enlightened focus of leadership shining into their work areas. Are they doing what they should be doing? If not, does someone notice and then provide them with what they need, from coaching to training to information?

A very large part of discipline consists simply of determination and courage. However, these alone are usually not enough to stand up to the pressures of a typical organization. No leader, however strong, can carry an entire organization on their back for long without structure and focus (and ownership). This is the beauty of Office Kaizen: It establishes a set of procedures through which the other three leadership parameters help create conditions that allow discipline to function without managers having to possess superhuman willpower.

DISCIPLINE WASTE

Whenever there is a failure of the system to react accurately and quickly to deterioration, neglect, or a problem, *discipline waste* occurs. This compromises the impact of focus and structure leadership efforts; nothing is as confusing to employees as unpredictable responses from the organization. If the employees have doubts as to what will happen if they take action, they will wait (surface waste) until a pattern is clear. If no pattern presents itself, they will do whatever they think is best (often leading to standardization and suboptimization surface waste). The following statements, if answered "false" by employees in a work group, are an indication of discipline waste:

1. My work group's lead person (supervisor, manager, and so on) meets at least four times a year with each person to discuss their performance, their joint expectations, and the work group's performance and goals.

2. Our supervisor (lead person, manager, and so on) meets with the work group regularly (at least once a week) to review group performance, results, and future expectations.

3. It is uncommon for members of my work group to miss commitments to others in the work group.

4. Data on our group's performance is accurate and/or up-to-date.

5. When our work area has a process problem, it is addressed quickly.

6. When our group comes up with an improvement, we are expected to take responsibility for running with it as far as we can.

7. When there is a process problem with another work group, it is dealt with quickly, openly, and effectively by the appropriate level of personnel.

8. My work group works effectively at encouraging optimum behaviors and performance among its members.

9. People in my work group appreciate advice and improvement suggestions from others in the group.

10. I have confidence that upper management is working hard to remove cross-functional barriers that compromise the productivity of my work group.

OWNERSHIP

What do you have if you have only minimized focus, structure, and discipline waste? You have a prison camp. You can make people do things with focus, structure, and discipline but you cannot engage their spirit without *ownership*. Human beings come "hard wired" from the factory with several behavioral mandates and many tendencies. One of the most powerful compulsions in people is a need to take ownership of things that are important to them. In most organizations, the existing, mostly informal, focus, structure, and discipline parameters work against allowing employees to exercise ownership of their work, work area, and processes.

Think about how most managers would react to the discovery that a group of workers is spontaneously rearranging their cubicles. Even though it has almost nothing to do with the employees' work processes, management would probably react as if they had been jabbed in the eye with a red-hot poker. Even though it is the employees' work area, management in most organizations believes that it "owns" the area, the processes, the outputs, and, yes, even the employees. This is the inevitable consequence of normal human and group dynamics operating within a traditional management structure. Unless there are intense feelings of ownership on the part of employees, a large portion of the potential surface waste reduction created by focus, structure, and discipline will be squandered. With good focus, structure, and discipline, an organization is poised for tremendous improvements in waste reduction (and in most other areas of productivity as well). Yet, without a sense of ownership, something will be missing at the most fundamental level.

Surface waste is most apparent at the level of work groups. These work groups must aggressively and enthusiastically attack surface waste within their areas every day in order for the organization to create a strategic competitive advantage. This requires self-generated, internally fueled enthusiasm and pride. This comes only from ownership. Focus, structure, and discipline set the stage, but ownership lights the fire that gets big results. Without cultivation of ownership within an organization, focus, structure, and discipline operate as they might in a well-run prison. The workers will do only what is required to stay out of trouble. They will not be encouraged or permitted to do more, because control is more important than output. In a non-prison setting, more than a minimum amount of control interferes with ownership.

It is leadership's role to make it possible for each employee to readily establish ownership over their processes and work area. Employee ownership of processes and outputs is the "secret" of all world-class leadership.

OWNERSHIP WASTE

Each time that an opportunity to increase employee ownership of their work area is not taken, *ownership waste* occurs. A strong culture of ownership can be found within a work group where the people answer most of the following statements as *true*:

1. I feel that the performance of my work group directly reflects upon me.

2. I feel comfortable bringing up quality, performance, and cost issues within the work group and with my supervisor (lead person, manager, and so on).

3. My work group has made many significant improvements in its day-to-day work processes.

4. There is a lot of peer pressure in the group to compel people to work together and do the best they can.

5. My work group has a formal system to capture and track improvement suggestions within the work group.

6. My work group is recognized as one that takes great pride in trying new ways to do things.

7. My work group and our supervisor (lead, manager, and so on) work together as a team to determine the best way to do things.

8. Our supervisor expects us to handle many minor and some major problems on our own.

9. My work group takes pride in its achievements.

10. I have no doubt that my work group is getting better all the time.

Remember, the goal of reducing leadership wastes is to enable the installation and operation of a system that reduces surface wastes and then continuously reduces them in order to establish a strategic competitive advantage. Attempting to resolve the issues behind "false" answers to the true or false statements presented in this chapter would create a complicated series of tactical, strategic, and even philosophical issues. Office Kaizen cuts to the chase and implements a system that slowly begins to increase the probability of a "true" answer to all 40 statements presented by the four leadership wastes.

Leaders must lead the entire organization for which they are responsible, not just a program, a department, a function, or a process. Office Kaizen is concerned primarily with creating a competitive advantage via the reduction of surface waste. It creates an environment and set of practices in which all leadership and management activities will begin to evolve toward world-class practice, whether the issue is technology, personnel selection, or marketing. A leader cannot practice and coach Office Kaizen in one dimension of his or her job without beginning to use its principles to reduce leadership waste in all endeavors. The next chapter will show why this comprehensive approach is absolutely essential for success, whether implementing Office Kaizen, merging two organizations, or introducing a new product.

5

Getting Human Nature on Your Side

George was excited but puzzled. Leadership waste certainly explains a lot of the problems at Biginslow and everywhere else I've worked, he thought. In fact, he realized that he and his executive team had not done anything to impose a consistent management structure on Biginslow. "And let's not even talk about discipline," he thought ruefully, "we always get bored with a project after the initial hoopla fades." He wondered why smart, aggressive, motivated managers and workers hadn't used logic to eliminate leadership wastes long ago. He wondered if there was something else at work, perhaps hidden forces that were stronger than simple logic.

Many change efforts fail because leaders mistakenly assume that normal business logic, planning, and rational thought are the most important variables in the success formula. While these factors are obviously important, shortfalls in them are not the reason why change efforts, large or small, fail. Efforts fail because leaders do not compensate for the realities of human behavior. Human behavior in organizations of any kind is driven by powerful, inexorable forces that cannot be ignored. If properly regulated and directed, these forces provide the supercharging boost that takes an organization from average to world-class. If these forces are ignored or improperly regulated, they generate confusion, friction, leadership waste, and surface waste.

In short, the failure to deal with the realities of human behavior is responsible for most business problems, failures, and shortfalls that are controllable by the organization. The consequences of these unrestrained forces create the default traditional status of most organizations. Organizations that are doing better than average over the long term have either consciously planned to control these forces or have stumbled upon part of the answer by luck. Office Kaizen is designed to explicitly bring these titanic forces to bear on the issues that are critical to management. This chapter describes what leaders are up against when trying to move an organization or a group from one set of behaviors to another.

ORGANIZATIONAL CULTURE AND INDIVIDUAL BEHAVIOR

Many people speak of organization culture and cultural change as if they are secret, mysterious processes that are understood only by specialists. There is nothing mysterious about the mechanics of corporate culture other than the extent to which the concept is used to promote poorly focused change management approaches. Culture is simply behavior that is supported, expected, reinforced, and valued by a group of people over a long period of time. Culture need not be more complicated.

When a person performs a behavior, such as pointing out a problem in a meeting, four elements of the behavior occur at once:

1. *Action*—This is the physical movement of the body. In this case, it would be the employee standing up and saying, "I think the problem is caused by late reporting of the budget variances each week."

2. *Thought*—This is whatever is going through the employee's mind, "*I shouldn't say anything, but I can't just sit here.*"

3. *Emotion*—This is whatever the employee is feeling. In this case it might be nervousness, a bit of fear, and excitement.

4. *Physiological Changes*—These are the changes in heart rate, GSR (sweating), EKG, hormones, EEG, and so on.

The only one of the four components of behavior that is under the constant, reliable, direct control of a person's consciousness is action. Few people can control their thoughts, emotions, and physiological responses without extensive training and practice. Just try, with your eyes closed, to think of nothing but a single word, like "meatball" (readers in California may prefer to think of the word "tofu"). If you are not highly skilled in meditation, your mind will wander.

The same principles apply to changing the behavior of others. Consider what is involved in getting employees to pay more attention to "quality." A common approach is to have a meeting and present a lot of data about quality, competitors, customers' requirements, and market behavior. Often, the rational appeal is augmented by a "Let's win one for the Gipper" speech from an executive. The intent is to encourage employees to think and/or be emotionally charged up about quality, so they will go out and "do something" about it.

Behavior changes (new actions with accompanying thoughts) rarely occur by presenting people with new thoughts and/or appealing to their emotions. They may listen, believe, and become excited, but then they are thrown right back into the old environment with a massive set of rewards, expectations, and rituals that support the existing actions. The thoughts and fleeting emotions don't have a chance. One time in a thousand, a "burning bush" phenomenon occurs in which an employee sees the light of the new way and becomes a zealot for the new thoughts. However, most of the time the employee is either slowly deprogrammed by the existing culture or becomes a figure of ridicule, an outcast to whom nobody listens as they rant on at every meeting about "the issue."

The bottom line is this: to change behaviors, focus must be turned to changing actions first. There is no other way. Office Kaizen is designed to change actions and keep them changed long enough for them to become new behaviors (actions backed up by supporting thoughts and emotions). How does one continuously change a stream of small actions on the part of many people and keep them changed? This is where the inborn tendencies of human beings come into play. If approached correctly, the fundamental nature of human beings will work to help create these small changes and reward them. The same forces that destroy most change efforts can be harnessed to an organization's benefit.

People are equipped from birth with a number of hard-wired tendencies, preferences, and needs. These predilections are the same for all healthy people in the world. Society, the summed operation of these tendencies, preferences, and needs modified by the local environment, then goes to work and teaches each person to behave in certain ways. Insofar as issues such as seeking approval, valuing children, seeking status, feeling shame, wanting to be recognized for one's achievements, respecting authority, and so on, are involved, every society in the world is so close to identical in what they teach that the differences are only of value to anthropologists. We will briefly examine a number of these hard-wired human tendencies and evaluate: 1) the impact they have on traditionally-run organizations (where they are poorly controlled); and 2) how they operate in organizations that have implemented Office Kaizen (where the full power of these forces is harnessed by leadership).

CONTROL THEORY: THE FIVE NEEDS THAT DRIVE ALL HUMAN BEHAVIOR

Control theory nicely summarizes the factors that drive us to act from minute to minute, day to day, and year to year. Control theory posits the five inborn needs of:

1. *Survival/Reproduction.* This is the need to stay alive and reproduce. This need has kept humans alive, procreating, and interested in their own welfare through at least 100,000 years of harsh, primitive conditions. At work, it is essential that employees be able to "see" how their day-to-day actions directly influence their survival. They must see data and relate it to their jobs.

2. *Belonging/Love.* This is the need to be part of a group that provides an opportunity to be personally valued by significant others.

3. *Power.* This is the need to influence the surrounding environment. This is what drove the development of the first tools (and all technology since then).

4. *Freedom.* This is the need to make choices on one's own.

5. *Fun.* This is the need for childlike play to diffuse tension. Fun is critical because each person is trying to get as much survival/reproduction, power, and freedom for him/herself as possible while remaining in a group environment in order to meet belonging/love needs.

An important point is that all people have the same basic set of needs: the approach that works for one person will work more or less (within a narrow range) for everyone else. An even more critical insight for management is to realize that people do not care whether the need satisfaction is good for the organization or not. An employee can just as well get a sense of belonging and love satisfaction by identifying with the self-reinforcing poison of the whiners and complainers as by trying to fight for continuous improvement. As long as the satisfaction is provided, the employee will take it, all other things being equal. The challenge to management is to assure that there are ample opportunities for employees to satisfy their needs by doing things that benefit the organization. If these are not available, employees will satisfy their needs by doing things that at worst hurt the organization or, at best, waste employee effort.

In a traditional organization, employees are typically left to their own devices to obtain need satisfaction. Very little structured effort is expended to create an environment in which the basic needs can be met in ways that help the organization attain its objectives. High turnover, union involvement, and indifference are only some of the consequences of a failure to systematically provide opportunities for obtaining need satisfaction for employees that also help the organization. In an Office Kaizen organization, each small work group is provided with focused and structured opportunities for satisfaction of all of the inborn needs.

INVOLVEMENT AND COMMITMENT

There is a hard-wired relationship between *involvement* and *commitment* in humans and many animals. If people are involved in something, they will be more committed to it. A committed person cares about the issue or activity, works to see that it is successful, and identifies with the results. There are two important points to keep in mind: 1) the involvement must include action, not just thought or emotion (people do not develop commitments to new thoughts, because there is interference from other, contradictory actions); and 2) it does not matter if the people like or dislike the actions they perform. It is better, of course, if they like them, but they will reinforce themselves either way.

In a traditional organization, there is much discussion and emotional exhortation, but few actual changes in action are required. As a result, it is difficult to get employees to perform new behaviors; the old actions maintain their strength. An even bigger problem is that no new set of actions is comprehensively required from a large portion of the organization, so there is little basis for establishing consistent rewards and expectations to permit the new action to overcome old actions. In an Office Kaizen organization, employees are focused and structured into performing a series of new, small actions that are relevant to their duties and work areas. Since these actions are supported by management (with their own new, small actions), there is a critical mass of people involved to provide sufficient rewards for new actions.

SMALL GROUP FORMATION

Human beings form small groups. The ideal size limit for a group is seven, plus or minus two (7±2). This is partly because we cannot communicate effectively with each person in groups that are larger than nine. A smaller group than five may not have enough psychological energy to overcome severe problems. A 7±2 group is the optimum size for managing communications and allowing all members to feel as if they are important to the group. When more people are added to a 7±2 group, the group will tend to split into two or three smaller groups. This can even happen to poorly run groups smaller than 7±2. This subgroup formation occurs whether management sees or sanctions it. Over time, the subgroups will come to have different views of the world, different procedures for doing the same work, and, typically, increasingly negative views about the other subgroups.

In a traditional organization, it is routine for a section or department to have 15 to 200 people and be considered a team. These groups splinter into informal, 7±2 groups that can provide the basic inborn needs, especially the need for belonging that only a small group can provide. Office Kaizen mandates work groups of 7±2 (except when the minimum size is constrained to less than five) so that it is easy for employees to work together and provide each other with need satisfaction.

CONFORMITY

People *conform* by displaying behaviors that are expected and rewarded. The expectation may not be voiced and the reward may be nothing more than no bad consequences; but expectations/feedback always exist, and they are powerful. After all, there is probably no policy that prohibits hourly employees in an organization from seeking an appointment with the CEO to discuss continuous improvement. Few do, because they know they would be violating the expectations of supervisors, coworkers, and probably the CEO. Conversely, few managers feel comfortable serving as a working team member on a problem-solving team when the leader of the team and the other members are hourly employees. It violates too many expectations. Human beings do not want to look bad to people they care about.

The most powerful influence on most people is their work group. They know that if they do not give the group what it wants, they risk their belonging need satisfaction (or more). If the person they want to keep happy is an authority figure who expects certain behaviors, they risk survival need satisfaction (they may get fired) if the authority figure is displeased. One only has to read the newspapers to see what stupid and horrible things people will do when they are part of a group. It is all driven by conformity.

In a traditional organization, little effort is expended to shift the expected behaviors that are the norm for the culture. The correct things are said, but expected actions are determined by the existing culture. In an Office Kaizen organization, every mechanism is designed to gradually shift the expected actions of everyone toward the world-class end of the spectrum.

SOCIAL LOAFING

As a group gets larger, there is increased probability that *social loafing* will occur. As the name implies, this means that individuals in the group will be inclined to throttle back on their efforts. As a group increases in number, it becomes more difficult for the members to participate fully with each other. As group intimacy decreases (and subgroups begin to form), the commitment to the original group is transferred to either the subgroup or some outside group or activity that becomes a more effective source of need satisfaction. With special training in group communications and teamwork, a group can hold social loafing at bay with as many as 12 people. With more than 12 people, social loafing and the formation of subgroups is inevitable.

In a traditional organization, sections, committees, teams, and departments are formed without regard to the impacts of social loafing and its effects on need satisfaction and commitment to the group. Also, if the individuals in the groups are not inclined to be as involved as they were in a smaller group, they will be less committed to group goals and expected behaviors. In an Office Kaizen organization, work group and change team size limits, as well as the mechanisms of the lean daily management system, tightly control social loafing.

AUTHORITY AND STATUS

Being social creatures, we create social structures. Every social structure on earth (those of bees, ants, primates, elephants, and so on) has a leader and a status hierarchy. A leader, by their simple presence, helps a group save energy and avoid trouble. With a leader in place, the non-leaders can spend more time surviving and reproducing, and the group wastes little energy fighting over who is in charge. This mechanism enabled groups of our ancestors to survive in a brutally unforgiving environment for tens of thousands of years. It is still within us. This means that there will always be various management levels and different privileges and responsibilities for each level, because we cannot deny our human mandate.

In a traditional organization, leaders assume that if nobody is complaining (too loudly), they are doing a good job and therefore they do not need to change much of what they do. Without an Office Kaizen structure in place, there is a great deal of variability between what various managers and management levels require of employees who wish to look good to their bosses. This variability creates all sorts of surface waste, including conflicting goals, suboptimization, friction, and cross-functional conflicts. Office Kaizen provides employees with a very detailed and objective description of what they must do to look good to management. Suddenly, all employees are working to curry favor with management in a way that serves the organization (and the employees and management).

POLARIZATION

Individuals in a group "polarize" their attitudes and beliefs, usually without being aware of it, to more closely reflect the expected behaviors the group has established. The more the individual values the group and/or its approval, the more the beliefs are polarized. The effect of *polarization* is to pull the extremes of opinion and perceptions back to the mean. Discrepant and divergent views are suppressed. Much data is lost. This is why it is dangerous to allow a group from a single department, process, or organizational level to make decisions that concern a larger part of the organization. One group's view is likely to be more homogenous and thus less diverse and less informed than good decision making requires. This is also why a single change agent, however zealous, usually "goes native" (comes to value what is important to others in the environment) when they are sent in from outside the organization to change things.

In a traditional organization, polarization is allowed to run rampant without structured efforts to mitigate its effects. Office Kaizen assures that representative groups address cross-functional and cross-process issues. Further, each team works with an approved charter (chapter 6) that minimizes the impact of the little bit of polarization that might occur.

COGNITIVE DISSONANCE

Cognitive dissonance occurs when our perceptual and intellectual expectations in a situation are not met. When this occurs, we are faced with several alternatives: 1) deny reality, 2) alter our interpretation of reality to match our expectations, or 3) alter our existing beliefs and knowledge to incorporate the new information. It is much easier to deny reality than to accept that we must change our expectations, beliefs, and need satisfaction paradigms. Regardless of which alternative we take, the choice does not occur at a conscious level. Cognitive dissonance occurs at a subconscious, neural-emotional level of processing. The instant that our conditioned, habitual expectations are not met, our minds make an automatic adjustment, usually subconsciously.

The difficulty is the processing that occurs on the part of large numbers of employees every day in regard to changes that leadership wants. Without focus, structure, and discipline behind the new actions that are desired, the employees are going to go with either option one or two. In other words, cognitive dissonance is continually pulling everyone toward the average of the existing culture. The impacts are horrendous and comprehensive. It is assumed that if something overt and objective is not occurring, the organization is in neutral culture mode while it waits for management to take a bold step. The existing culture is always being reinforced by employees responding with option one. When a bold initiative is finally launched, it runs into a concrete wall made up of millions of previous option one reinforcements.

Office Kaizen creates a wide-ranging series of small, new actions. Each one has some, but only a little, discrepancy from what is expected. Most employees respond with options two or three. As more actions change and are supported by employees, the dissonance between expected and perceived continually drops. Eventually, most employees respond with option three to any required action changes.

WHAT DO THESE TENDENCIES CREATE?

When allowed to function without Office Kaizen, the tendencies described above create a traditional work environment. The traditional work environment is the default setting for all human organizations on Earth; it is what happens when nature takes its course. It is true for schools, businesses, community groups, religious groups, government agencies, political parties, and nonprofit organizations. This is why so few world-class organizations are created spontaneously. In order to get world-class performance over time, the traditional, default human organization must be replaced by a system that operates in the same manner as Office Kaizen.

In the traditional default organization, people obtain considerable rewards for doing work that is often not in the best long-term interests of the organization. These rewards come from themselves, peers, and bosses, each of whom is also struggling to get their needs met in an organization where conformity, cognitive dissonance, status striving, and the like are operating uncontrolled. Some of the "happy" work that provides the most rewards for employees includes work that:

- Makes their work group look good

- Is interesting

- Is fun

- Is easy

- Reinforces their own self image

- Is what they do best

- Avoids conflicts they don't want

- Creates conflicts they enjoy

- Covers up their shortfalls

- Keeps coworkers happy

- Is understood the most

- Gives them a sense of accomplishment

- Keeps them out of trouble

- Is pleasing to their boss

Unfortunately, there are few jobs, if any, in which a worker doing only the above types of work would be doing a good job for the organization. Sometimes it is necessary to rock the boat. Yet, rocking it too much and too often causes trouble. Without Office Kaizen, employees in traditional organizations are surviving on what little satisfaction they can get by doing the "happy" work, while knowing they should be doing the "less pleasant" work that:

- Makes their work area look bad (acknowledging a problem)

- Is boring (tracking inventory)

- Is unpleasant (administering discipline or updating procedures)

- Makes them look bad to the group (fewer errors)

- Exposes their weaknesses (acknowledging a problem)

- Aggravates their co-workers (focused and productive)

- Is understood the least (year-end budget projections)

- Provides no sense of achievement (daily reports and logs)

- Forces them to fight the system (timely responses)

- Does not like to be seen by their boss (employee-level problem resolutions)

If an employee does not get a lot of support to do the correct and rational "unpleasant" work that must be done, they will go with the cultural flow and fall back quickly to the immediate and almost-guaranteed rewards that "happy" work provides. The key to creating a world-class organization is, as far as possible, to transform "unpleasant" work into "happy" work. Office Kaizen does this by installing a new set of expected actions that provides immediate need satisfaction both from management and from an employee's work group when they perform a necessary, previously "unpleasant" work action. In effect, all work becomes necessary work that has focus, structure, discipline, and ownership and provides need satisfaction that is good for the organization, management, and the employee.

6

The Concept of SLIM-IT and the Structure of Change

George smiled as if he had just gotten his stock option package for a record-setting year. "No wonder all of our previous efforts to move toward world-class produced only a nudge or two," exclaimed George. "The programs were not designed to comprehensively address leadership wastes and change behavior. They were collections of tools and technologies that didn't do anything much to deal with the biggest forces that were resisting change. It's easy to see why so many efforts fail."

He sat for several minutes thinking of all the continuous improvement coordinators that were running around the organization. They were doing great things but were only moving a few pieces of a few processes in the right direction. He recalled that presentation last month in the customer service center of the Acme Mega Lease Corporation. He was showing the flag and traveling to a succession of continuous improvement pitches. A great reengineering effort had been done on channeling customer service calls to the right people. Yet, right in the area, at the same time, he had found outdated procedures posted and being used by representatives to authorize adjustments. ("And I don't even know that much about the operation," he thought. "What would I have found if I knew what to look for?") And, none of the employees he asked had any idea of how their success was being

> measured. "One thing's for sure," he thought, "if Office Kaizen
> isn't the answer to the problem, I don't know what else could be."
> George continued reading, now intent on learning exactly how
> Office Kaizen works.

THE CONCEPT OF SLIM-IT

Office Kaizen is the system that influences everything that happens in a world-class organization in which leadership wastes are being minimized. It is the way in which people, processes, tools, approaches, actions, culture, market pressures, organization dynamics, customer demands, shareholder expectations and human needs interact to produce a strategic competitive advantage. *SLIM-IT is the tactical approach and primary engine of any Office Kaizen (or any other) implementation, because it aggressively attacks the leadership wastes that derail so many initiatives and creates a culture of continuous, sustainable improvement.* Office Kaizen is the result and SLIM-IT is the method for getting started and maintaining the necessary structure over the long term.

Figure 6.1 presents a high-level conceptual representation of SLIM-IT. SLIM-IT is a pronunciation of the acronym for Structure, Lean daily management system (or LDMS*), Mentoring, Metrics and Tools, Teamwork, Training, and Technology. These terms yield SLMMTTTT, pronounced "SLIM-IT." The central portion of the figure, displayed in white, indicates elements that are typical to all organizations, that is, "normal business operations."

The world-class challenge is to "run the business" (the center of Figure 6.1) better than the competition. Increasingly, the "competition" is not simply others in the same industry but any organization in which shareholders can invest their money. This increases the urgency for pursuing Office Kaizen even in well-run organizations. "Running the business" is the usual operations, strategy, planning, marketing/sales, customer service, purchasing, design, and so on that must be conducted amidst the chaos of politics, human needs, world markets, unexpected problems, and the like. There are many items within the center of the figure, but the "T" in SLIM-IT refers to *tools, teamwork, training,* and *technology*—the four most commonly applied leverage points for fixing problems in traditional organizations.

---

*LDMS is a service mark of The Kaufman Consulting Group, LLC.

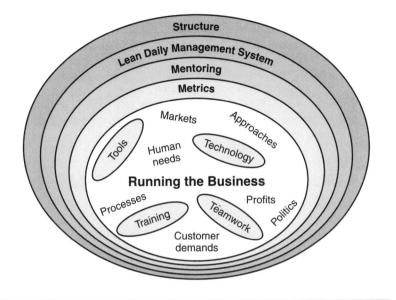

Figure 6.1   High-level conceptual diagram of the SLIM-IT model.

Most organizations have sufficient amounts of the "four Ts" within themselves (either latent or lying fallow) to achieve almost any objective, *if* they are applied in the right combination in the right amounts at the right times. This is very difficult to do on a consistent basis.

In an Office Kaizen environment, SLIM-IT focuses on two primary leverage points in an organization:

1. Reducing leadership wastes in the management of change initiatives

2. Reducing leadership wastes within every intact work group

SLIM-IT uses structure, the lean daily management system (LDMS), mentoring, and metrics to compel the right amounts of the four Ts (and everything else) to come together more often and in greater amounts than they do in a traditionally run organization. SLIM-IT does not transform an organization overnight, but a great many dramatic improvements will quickly become visible. World-class performance, as anyone who is already there will attest, takes a one to two percent, consistent change in critical actions by each employee on a daily basis over a long time.

Think of the structure, LDMS, mentoring, and metrics rings of the SLIM-IT model (Figure 6.1) as compression bands that force the items in the center to jostle, disturb, rub, bounce off of, grind up against, interact with, and jumble each other in close proximity. This results in the discovery of synergies and effective (and ineffective) combinations of resources that would never have been discovered without the compression. This chapter and the next few describe in detail the individual elements of SLIM-IT and how they work together to provide sufficient focus, structure, discipline, and ownership so that the best possible synergies are discovered, maintained, and continuously improved.

STRUCTURED CHANGE MANAGEMENT

An organization moves from a current state to a new one (better or worse) as a result of changes in critical parameters and functions. Some changes are driven quickly by outside forces in the industry (for example, mergers, new products/concepts), government/politics (for example, new regulations, regional conflicts, and taxes), and/or technology. Other changes occur slowly over time, unnoticed until results cannot be denied (for example, a slow erosion of competitiveness due to a failure to adjust to new market conditions). Finally, many changes are driven from within an organization, either in response to the above changes or to satisfy other needs (for example, installing a new computer system, integrating an acquisition's systems and personnel, moving a facility, or introducing a new product). The management of all changes in an organization must be focused, structured, disciplined, and owned by the involved personnel. The structure element of SLIM-IT meets these requirements through the use of an *executive steering committee, champions, charters, change teams,* and *change team leaders.*

Figure 6.2 provides a detailed, conceptual diagram of the *structural* element of SLIM-IT. Here, elements of SLIM-IT and Office Kaizen are shown in gray, and "normal" business operations are shown in white.

THE EXECUTIVE STEERING COMMITTEE

The central leadership element (and overall driver) of SLIM-IT is the executive steering committee (ESC). (The title of this group, as with all of the other labels used to describe the mechanics of SLIM-IT and Office Kaizen, can be changed as befits an organization's tastes and existing structures.) The ESC is the existing top-level management team at a site, office, or location (if there are not more than 10 or 12; a larger site management team will

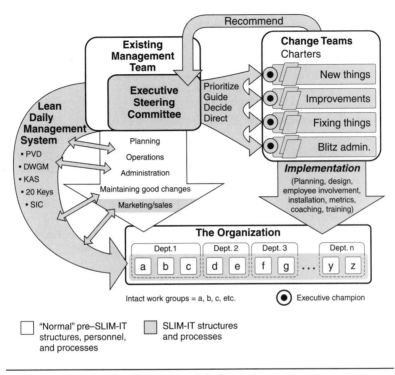

Figure 6.2 A detailed conceptual model of SLIM-IT.

need to pick a subset for the ESC, hence the less than total overlap shown in the diagram). The SLIM-IT model cannot do its job at the corporate level, although the corporate office could apply the model to its own site and staff. This does not imply that corporate executives do not have significant Office Kaizen implementation duties. They do, and they are critical to success in the discrete locations that report to them. Chapter 12 deals with this and other implementation issues.

The ESC should never be more than 10 to 12 people. It can violate the 7±2 optimal team size mandate a bit and not lose too much, as the ESC is more of a committee than a team. If there is a union, it is important to keep its representatives appraised and involved. If the relationship with the union is good, the highest elected official should be invited to be on the ESC. They may be forced by political necessity, even in a friendly environment, to decline. If this is the case, the site executive must offer to update the union executive in detail as to ESC activities as soon as possible after each ESC meeting. The intent is to slowly bring the union into the process as part of the solution, rather than force it through exclusion to be part of the problem.

The role of the ESC is to guide, prioritize, direct, focus, coach, counsel, and make decisions on critical change parameters. The ESC meets once a week at a predetermined time. (If a representative cannot attend, they must send a subordinate with decision-making authority.) One of the most important functions of the ESC is to compel the leadership team at a site to embrace and deal with the entire range of changes that are ongoing, including allocation of resources, priority setting, and achievement of objectives. The leadership team is responsible for leading change and the ESC structure allows them to be leaders of the site in the best sense of the word: directing, coaching, guiding, prioritizing, allocating, helping, and understanding the big picture. Through the participation of champions (explained below), certain leaders become intimate with the smaller, detailed picture of each effort.

ESC participation typically requires two to four hours per week per person. About an hour and a half is consumed by the weekly ESC meeting. The remainder of the time is used to champion various teams and handle behind-the-scenes politics with other ESC members and other managers. When an ESC is first formed, the first few weeks will require considerably more time as initiatives will have to be identified and many teams formed. The time devoted to the ESC will quickly free up a great deal of problem solving and emergency, firefighting time.

CHANGE TEAMS

A *change team* is formed by the ESC for any significant modification in the organization. A change is "significant" if it meets one or more of the following criteria:

1. Involves a large number of people (more than 10)

2. Involves more than "normal" day-to-day work processes

3. Is complex

4. Is cross-functional

5. Involves several levels (in terms of the management hierarchy)

6. Is technically difficult

7. Makes significant alternations in the way things are done

8. Will likely encounter significant resistance

As you can see from the above list, the typical organization launches many changes that do not have the benefit of a formally chartered team. This is a major source of leadership waste and resulting loss of productivity. In a facility with 200 to 500 people, it is not uncommon to discover 10 or 15 significant changes being implemented by a single manager or group of managers, with little or no involvement on the part of many of the people who will be impacted. Often, many effected managers know little or nothing about what is going on. Many times, the top-level manager of a site only gets involved in a critical initiative when its failure creates problems for the entire site. This is why chartered teams with ESC oversight and regular review are so critical to Office Kaizen.

A chartered team must be formed for corporate-driven initiatives as well. The change team will handle the site implementation after getting much of its charter content from the corporate materials. Each change team presents a short (no longer than 10 minutes) update as to how its efforts are going in the ESC meeting. It is imperative that the presentations be made by the team, the team leader, or a selected team member at the discretion of the team, rather than by a member of management. The updates must contain as few new materials as possible. It is vital that the presentations be pithy, brief updates rather than displays of PowerPoint virtuosity.

For purposes of descriptive accuracy, the various change teams can be divided into four categories:

1. *New things team*—Changes that implement an entirely new system (for example, a new software system) or process (for example, installing primary visual displays for intact work groups).

2. *Improvement team*—Changes to improve an existing system or process.

3. *Fixing things team*—Changes to correct flaws or problems (for example, a nagging problem with account follow-up on new business).

4. *Kaizen blitz team*—This team is a little different. It is a permanent team (with rotating membership) that plans and administers all of the intensive week-long blitz events at the site.

The difference between a team that fixes something and a team that improves things is a judgment call and is not critical; the names used here are intended to illustrate the purposes the teams serve. In fact, there may be a fuzzy line between new things and improvements when speaking of software upgrades. Most organizations use more "sophisticated" names for these teams (for example, continuous process improvement, reengineering implementation). The names of the teams are not as important (except for political impact) as the structure that guides them.

In general, team leaders and team members should be "doers," the people who do the actual work. One of the problems with many traditional change teams is the presence of supervisors and managers who attempt to direct the team and who do very little work themselves. The supervisors and managers should be running the business. The teams should be populated with the people who know the processes best: the hands-on workers. Depending upon the topic, a supervisor or two on the team is acceptable and perhaps even essential, but they should not be in a team leader role (unless the supervisor is a good leader and isn't afraid to get their hands dirty with the team's work). It is up to the team leader, the ESC (in the weekly review) and the team champion to make sure the team stays on track.

The kaizen administration team is rather unique. A *kaizen blitz* (or "reengineering blitz" or "continuous improvement event") is an intense, three- to five-day, full-time effort by a small group of three to six people (never more; although 10 people on two teams could work at the same time, thereby "doing" two kaizen events) to analyze and fix a specific part of a process or work area. A blitz is an effective way to get a "quick hit," or result. Blitzes do everything from changing office layouts to reengineering small pieces of processes to conducting clean-up events (for example, straightening files, labeling supplies, redesigning office layouts, and so on). Often, one or several blitzes will be conducted to support a longer-term change team such as a fixing things team. The blitz administration team that reports to the ESC is an administrative/coaching function responsible for selecting possible blitz targets, lining up personnel to "do" the blitz, and arranging for the blitz coach and blitz meeting room. The blitz administration team makes the preparations for the presentation of blitz results to a large group of managers and supervisors on the last day of the blitz. The blitz team is also responsible for making sure that loose ends from blitzes are tracked, assigned for completion, and continuously reviewed. The status of completed and pending blitzes is updated to the ESC each week by the blitz team.

Blitzes in general require a few additional comments. They are an outstanding way to improve operations, get a fast return on the investment of time and effort and demonstrate to everyone that "even this place can do incredible, good things fast." Every site in every business should have a blitz team (by whatever name) reporting to the ESC. Every site should have regular blitzes, if for no other reason than because a typical blitz adds an average of $100,000 to the bottom line if annualized over the next 12 months. A site with 100 people should do a blitz every four to six weeks. Locations with 200 people should conduct blitzes every three weeks. Sites with 500 to 1000 cannot afford *not* to do blitzes every two to three weeks.

All of the personnel on the teams doing the blitzes need not be from within the organization. Suppliers, customers, and even personnel from neighboring businesses can be invited to send a participant when the process/area is related to their interests. They represent free, eager help, and they learn a skill that strengthens their own organization and the economic viability of the community.

However, do not become intoxicated with blitzes. As wonderful and exciting as they are, they can be addictive if used recklessly by traditional managers. Blitzes appeal to the traditional side of management—management does little and gets a lot. Blitzes do nothing to attack the leadership waste that is at the heart of the issue. Blitzes are a powerful, useful, and absolutely necessary tool that must be employed on a regular basis. However, blitzes alone will not get an organization even close to world class.

CHAMPIONS

Each member of the ESC is required to be a *champion* of one or more of the teams. The champion must never be allowed to assist a team that is primarily engaged in an area or process that the champion controls and/or in which they are an expert. The champion's role is to coach the process, not come up with the answers. The champion works with the team to fine-tune its charter (explained below), helps the team leader select team members, assists the team by working with other managers behind the scenes, and provides ongoing coaching and guidance to the team as it works.

This participation in team activities is critical to both the teams and the champion. The teams need the visible, direct support of management. Each team will face tremendous pressures and will generally require a little management "backbone" to face down the resistance to change. The champion also benefits greatly, because with each new team they assist, they are reminded that completing any initiative is a brutal, hand-to-hand battle with bayonets, grenades, and small arms. This experience broadens and deepens the champion's understanding of how the organization works. This knowledge is a fundamental requirement for developing the insights necessary to lead an organization to world-class status.

CHARTERS

Each team develops a *charter* with the assistance and direction (and approval) of the ESC. A typical charter has the following elements:

1. *Mission* (general statement of purpose).

2. *Objectives* (specific goals to be attained).

3. *Names* of the team champion, team leader, and team members.

4. *Activities* to be completed (in chronological order).

5. *Responsibilities*—This is a matrix of the above activities and involved personnel that indicates an "R" (the people who are responsible; the "doers"), an "A" (those who are accountable; those at whom the buck finally stops), a "C" (those consulted or checked with before the activity is performed), or an "I" (the informed, who are told after the fact of the activity). This matrix is often called a "responsibility chart" or a RACI chart.

6. *Deliverables* (tangible proof of completion such as the "to be" process flow of a new purchasing process).

7. *Schedule* of activities and deliverables.

8. *Critical success factors* (conditions vital to success).

When a team is conceived, the ESC may have nothing but a loose mission statement ("fix purchasing"), a champion, and a candidate team leader in mind. The champion and the ESC then recruit the team leader, work with him/her to pick a team, and assist the team in developing a charter. The ESC approves the charter (with changes, perhaps) and the champions coach the team as it works. In other cases, the ESC might have an almost complete charter in hand when the team is formed. This is often the case when a corporate program arrives at the front door of a site. Nonetheless, the team must modify the charter to accommodate the details of implementation. These customizations by the team are essential for reducing ownership waste.

It is important that charters be kept as "low-tech" as possible. This does not mean that computers cannot be used. However, the more computers are used to generate schedules and create glossy PowerPoint documents about status, the less real project work will be done. The last thing any change team needs is people huddled over their keyboards instead of out working in the organization. Leadership wastes have never been substantially reduced by glossy presentations. It takes careful team selection, a good champion, detailed team coaching, ESC reviews, and charter development to produce an optimum change effort.

7

The Lean Daily
Management System

George closed his eyes, leaned back in his chair and took a deep breath. Clearly he was beginning to see why most of their previous initiatives fell short of the mark. There was never enough executive involvement. George sat upright and said out loud, "An ESC would have kept everyone on the right track." More times than he cared to admit, attempts to resolve problems had simply caused additional problems, because they were done within one department with no thought of the negative impact across the organization. He could even remember when he was a site manager and was guilty of the "stretching plate syndrome." He was always eager to champion any new corporate initiative. The problem was that he was often unaware of all that was going on in other areas, let alone the fact that he was taking on more than he could handle.

As George began reading the next chapter, he couldn't help but wonder where the company would be today if he had been "enlightened" a few years back.

The management of change in an organization requires the structural dimension of SLIM-IT, described in the last chapter. Yet, structure is not the primary basis by which Office Kaizen establishes a strategic competitive advantage. The largest contribution to competitive superiority comes from leveraging improvement at the intact work group level using the lean daily management system (LDMS). Figure 7.1 expands the left side of Figure 6.1 (page 65). The purpose of the LDMS is to provide focus, structure, discipline, and ownership within each discrete, intact work group in the organization.

As shown in Figure 7.1, the executive steering committee (ESC) does not operate the LDMS. While the ESC must install the LDMS at the start of an Office Kaizen implementation (via the procedures described in chapter 6), the operation of LDMS is "normal business." The LDMS, once installed, becomes part of the everyday work in each intact work group. The LDMS is a means for management to aggressively focus, structure, and discipline daily activities so that what is done and how it is done more closely aligns with leadership's objectives. At the same time, the LDMS turns the normal, usually suboptimizing operation of belonging need satisfaction, territoriality, cognitive dissonance, and conformity into a positive force for improving work group ownership and pride.

As the LDMS operates, it lifts all processes and tasks up the performance ladder a little bit at a time. The changes from day to day and even from week to week are sometimes so small that only the people in the work area can identify them. In other instances, the changes are obvious to everyone. Yet, no matter what the size or velocity of improvements within work

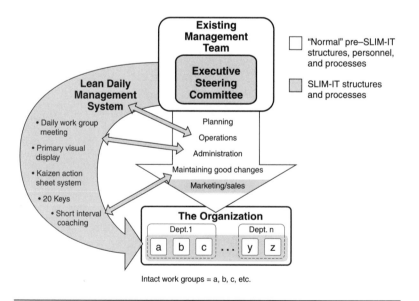

Figure 7.1   The lean daily management system element of SLIM-IT.

groups, the effect of the LDMS over time is profound and dramatic. Inexorably, the LDMS slowly ratchets the organization's performance above the level playing field of the competition. Suddenly, with only minimal contributions from bold, new ideas, the Office Kaizen organization has a strategic competitive advantage that is built upon small improvements in hundreds to thousands of individual performances, processes, and tasks.

The ultimate irony is that the Office Kaizen organization then further extends its competitive advantage by better implementing bold, new innovations. Moreover, when an Office Kaizen organization implements major initiatives, even when it is one that a competitor discovered first, the Office Kaizen organization always gets it done faster, more effectively, and with less cost and less disruption. This is because the LDMS relieves the management team of most of a traditional organization's daily burden of after-the-fact firefighting. An added benefit is that the leadership of an Office Kaizen organization has the time, resources, and patience to carefully explore and plan additional new ideas that will benefit their organization the most.

INTACT WORK GROUPS: THE FOCUS OF THE LDMS

The LDMS operates within intact work groups in the organization. An *intact work group* is a collection of individuals who perform tasks on similar, related, or connected processes in reasonably close physical proximity for most of their workday. Each intact work group installs its own LDMS (as this is the most fundamental level of the organization at which leadership wastes must be reduced—this is where the surface waste virus hides). Examples of intact work groups include:

- The nine people in a human resources office
- Seven purchasing representatives in a materials department
- The nine administrative assistants that support an organization's corporate executives
- A seven-person sales office
- The four people in the benefits area of a large human resources office
- Eight people in a claims processing department
- The four lawyers in a legal department
- The entire nine-person shift of a fast food outlet

- Five engineers working on a new product development effort

- Seven people in a manufacturing work cell

- Each of five work groups (7±2 people each) in a large call center

- The five members of a corporate relations department

- The six legal aides that support the tax attorneys in a law firm

The above intact work groups share and/or swap work, substitute for one another on occasion, have many of the same problems, and can benefit from the insights and expertise of each other. In cases where an intact work group has more than 7±2 members, the group must be split. This does not mean that the work group must be reorganized in terms of titles, responsibilities, or tasks. The sole reason for the absolute necessity of applying the LDMS to teams of less than 10 was discussed in chapter 5: the 7±2 limit on effective group size.

Not all groups are intact work groups. The management team of an organization is not an intact work group (it is more like a committee), because its members do not work in close proximity for most of the day on similar tasks. Some middle managers and technical personnel easily fit into an intact work group; others do not. Do not force a fit if one is not there.

ELEMENTS OF THE LDMS

The LDMS is comprised of five elements. They are:

1. Daily work group meeting

2. Primary visual display (PVD)

3. Kaizen action sheet (KAS) system

4. Short-interval leadership

5. KCG 20 Keys* assessment and long-term improvement plan

Daily Work Group Meeting

Definition—The work group meeting is a mandatory, short, daily meeting on company time of each intact work group in front of the work group's primary visual display board.

---

*KCG 20 Keys is a registered trademark of The Kaufman Consulting Group, LLC.

Purpose—The daily work group meeting performs several very critical functions that cannot be provided through any other mechanism:

1. It brings the work group together as a team, even if the workers do not see themselves as a team (few work groups function as real teams). The physical act of coming together for a short meeting once a day will compel them to become a team (through cognitive dissonance) after a few weeks.

2. It provides every person in the work group with the same picture of what is going on.

3. It focuses each person on the metrics and key performance indicators that are critical to management.

4. It generates a sense of ownership among the team about its area, its processes, and its functions.

5. It provides an opportunity for supplying all of the basic needs satisfaction discussed in chapter 5 (survival, power, fun, freedom, and belonging).

Operation—The meetings must be stand-up meetings held in front of the group's primary visual display (described below). The standing is critical, because it is a deliberate action, unlike sitting. When people are standing as a group, it's hard for them to deny they are part of the group. After a number of meetings, cognitive dissonance pressures force the individuals into the fold of the team. The meetings must be short, never more than 10 minutes in length. They must be tightly facilitated to prohibit complaining, problem solving, and the like.

People often ask if conducting daily work group meetings less than every day is sufficient. The answer is NO, never. If a leader cannot afford to devote five to 10 minutes a day in each work group as an investment toward a strategic competitive advantage, they will not have the courage, insight, determination, and endurance to make any of the elements of Office Kaizen work. If the work group meetings were to be held only three times a week, it would take at least three times as long to establish a foundation and the results would be much, much slower in coming. Further, once the meetings go to three per week, who is to say that on a very busy week, it would not be okay to have only two? Mandate daily meetings, make managers patrol them, and walk in the well-policed sunlight of success.

Daily work group meetings are usually conducted by a trained supervisor or lead who then trains someone else to take over. After a few people are trained to lead the meetings, the group is one step closer to being a "self-managed" work group. The meetings' content must include a CNN-type

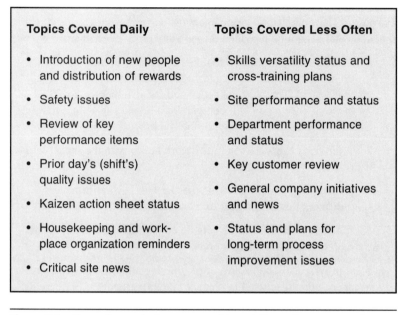

Topics Covered Daily	Topics Covered Less Often
• Introduction of new people and distribution of rewards	• Skills versatility status and cross-training plans
• Safety issues	• Site performance and status
• Review of key performance items	• Department performance and status
• Prior day's (shift's) quality issues	• Key customer review
• Kaizen action sheet status	• General company initiatives and news
• Housekeeping and work-place organization reminders	• Status and plans for long-term process improvement issues
• Critical site news	

Figure 7.2 General agenda items covered in a daily work group meeting.

overview of what happened the day (or shift) before, critical issues, what is planned for today, and a number of other brief items. Some items are reviewed every day (such as quality problems) while others are discussed only once a month. An agenda for the general structure of daily work group meetings is shown in Figure 7.2.

Primary Visual Display (PVD)

Definition—The PVD is a large (for example, four by eight feet to three by six feet; never smaller), two-dimensional information center that is updated as required. It displays all of the information discussed during the daily work group meeting.

Purpose—The PVD is the physical embodiment of the work group's spirit and pride. There is no computerized, high-tech substitute for having the entire group stand before the PVD and see the same thing in no uncertain terms at the same time. The intention is to have the group come to view the movement of key indicators as a direct reflection of their power, freedom, survival, and belonging needs satisfaction. Since they are making the indicators "move" through their own efforts, they begin to see the PVD as representative of their value and worth, not only to the organization, but to themselves as thinking, involved, creative human beings.

Operation—The PVD must be displayed in the work area so that it is amidst the workers during the day. This makes it easier to update, of course, but more importantly, it puts the content of the PVD front and center in everyone's focus. The PVD must be maintained daily. Someone has to be trained and assigned to do this. The first person to maintain the PVD in an area is usually the supervisor or the lead. Others are then trained. A new things team for a site designs (and gets the ESC to approve) the general format for the PVD and the procedures for getting people trained to maintain it.

It is critical that the PVD and daily work group meetings be scrupulously maintained. If they are not, the work groups will quickly lose respect for the entire process. Once the new things team completes the one- to three-week training period (for about 30 to 60 minutes per day) in an intact work group, this responsibility falls directly on the shoulders of the normal management team. Upper management, in their dual, overlapping role as ESC members and site leaders, must patrol the intact work groups and *compel* (coach, guide, advise, and, if necessary, reproach) them to maintain their PVD and meetings.

Kaizen Action Sheet (KAS) System

Definition—The KAS system is a method for capturing small improvement suggestions within each intact work group.

Purpose—The purpose of the KAS system is threefold:

1. To collect the little ideas that fall "below the radar" (and cost return requirements) of a site or companywide suggestion program

2. To provide the intact work group members with an opportunity to obtain power and freedom needs satisfaction by coming up with ways to make things better in their work area (as well as the belonging need satisfaction given to them by other group members for each suggestion)

3. To provide a means to identify and capture the little changes that eliminate surface waste at its source

Operation—The KAS is a single page form that a group member uses to submit a suggestion to the work group. Organizations change the name of the form to suit their own tastes. The suggestion is handwritten (never computerized; this wastes time). The KAS has three small boxes across the top half of the sheet. On the left is a small box in which to write a sentence describing the issue (for example, "it is difficult to find the proper code numbers for invoices"). In the middle is a box for the employee to write what they think should be done (for example, "create and place a list of the more common numbers at each desk"). The right box is used to write what they believe the result will be (for example, "fewer mistakes").

The bottom half of the sheet is two large boxes. The left one is used to draw a "before" picture, and the right box is used to draw an "after" picture, or what the employee believes the implemented suggestion looks like. The drawings are mistakenly omitted on many organizations' adaptations of the KAS. The reason why it is a mistake is yet another lesson as to why it is important for leaders to understand how and why human beings behave. A powerful part of creating commitment to an idea is compelling the person who fills out the KAS to think about the idea enough to feel a strong sense of ownership. Drawing separate before and after pictures, however crude, is critical to this ownership.

People think with both hemispheres of the brain. The left side is used for logical, sequential, and verbal reasoning. The right side is used for symbolic, creative, and nonlinear thinking. Everyone uses both sides, of course, but most people are inclined more to one side than the other (for example, lawyers tend to be "lefties," and artists tend to be "righties"). By requiring an employee to both write their idea and draw it, their entire brain is involved and they are forced to think about other aspects of the problem. In the case of the example above, the "before" picture might be an unhappy face looking at an empty spot on a desk. The "after" picture might be a happy face with a piece of paper next to it. It doesn't sound like much, but it is one of the subtle little things that are important.

The KAS system operates through four folders on the primary visual display. From left to right or top to bottom, they are labeled: 1) Blank Forms, 2) Submitted, 3) Working, and 4) Resolved. An employee with a suggestion completes a blank form and places it in the "submitted" folder. Within 24 to 72 hours (a policy set at the site by the ESC), the person leading the daily work group meetings must disposition the submitted suggestion in front of the group. The meeting leader announces it to the group (for example, "Allison put in a suggestion to develop a list of key account numbers") and then does one of the following:

1. Says that they will "handle it" and get back to them

2. Asks if anyone else would like to "handle it"

3. Assigns someone to "handle it"

4. Turns it down

5. Says that it is too "big" (cross-functional or resource intensive) and that they will take it to the ESC for possible action

It is essential to focus the group's generation of ideas on low-tech solutions that they can do themselves. It is too easy for most work groups to blame their problems on lack of software, technology, money, or personnel. The entire purpose of the LDMS (and Office Kaizen) is to attain a competitive advantage from the massed effects of thousands of small, low-tech sources. This means that in the above example, the list of code numbers would be put on a piece of paper, copied, and then placed at each desk, perhaps in a plastic, protective sleeve. It would not be submitted as a software request to have the code numbers put into a pop-up menu on each person's computer screen. This might be the appropriate downstream action in a year or two, but it is a disastrous short-term solution. A computer support request would take months to process, be costly, require dozens of hours of support from the intact work group, and encourage the intact work group to depend upon others to make its work better. Even worse, the idea may not work. Over a few months to a year, the work group tests and optimizes the solution. If a site-wide coding system is needed, it should come from the ESC, not a work group (every work group is, of course, free to forward ideas to the ESC through supervisors, managers, champions, and mentors).

Once a KAS is completed or found to be impractical, it is moved to the "resolved" folder. Do not permit anyone to computerize a list of the KAS. If a list is computerized, it will not be long before site management and then corporate management requires status reports on KAS "productivity." Massive amounts of time and resources will be wasted. Do not collect them, list them, or send them to other sites as "lessons learned" or best practices. The "best practice" that should be promulgated is installation of the LDMS and the KAS system. Each intact work group at other sites has plenty of its own ideas that will surface within its own KAS system.

There is a tendency, when the KAS system is first installed in a traditional work group, for employees to generate considerable numbers of ideas that require information system support and/or the purchase of equipment. It is imperative that every work group be told that there will be no large expenditures or extensive systems work done in a work group until that intact work group attains 50 points on the KCG 20 Keys (which will be described in chapter 9). This will compel each intact work group to explore low-tech solutions (thus taking control of their destiny with actions they can control). By the time a work group attains 50 points, most of the big expenditures it would have suggested earlier will not be necessary or desired. The only exception to this guideline, of course, would be safety or customer quality issues. Critical, large expenditures and/or requests for extensive systems support can always originate from change teams reporting to the executive steering committee.

Short-Interval Leadership

Definition—Short-interval leadership is periodic, regular contact by the supervisor or lead with each employee within an intact work group.

Purpose—The purpose of short-interval leadership is fivefold:

1. To check on the status of key parameters

2. To determine if prior problems have been resolved

3. To provide an opportunity for each employee to get support or report problems without "being a pest" or having to leave their work area or remember the problem for the next daily work group meeting

4. To create the reality in each employee's perception that "the system" cares about and takes action on the little things

5. To provide the employee with opportunities for power and freedom need satisfaction

Operation—Short-interval leadership requires that a lead person or supervisor visit each employee within the intact work group at least twice a day for 15 to 30 seconds. If there is a problem, the lead or supervisor writes it down and checks it out. They report the status at the next visit or at the following day's work group meeting. If the group or a particular person is experiencing severe problems, the visits might be as often as once every hour or two for several weeks. Since there is a maximum of less than 10 people in each intact work group, the burden is not severe.

Many managers contend that resources are not available to do such "visiting." Quite simply, an organization cannot afford *not* to do short-interval leadership. The alternative is to allow small problems to fester into profit-destroying disasters. As with daily work group meetings, a large portion of short-interval leadership can be allocated to those who are trained. They need not be formal supervisors or leads. Such duties can be made into a badge of honor or defined as an intermediate next step (for example, "All new supervisors will be selected only from those who have been trained and are skilled at conducting daily meetings and short-interval leadership duties"). These are the sorts of processes that are the essence of what happens in self-managed work groups (also known as self-directed teams, empowered work groups, and so on).

To make the most of the short-interval leadership process, each person in the intact work group must have a checklist or form upon which problems can be noted. This captures, in real time, information on small issues that might not seem like a big deal two to four hours later when the short-interval leadership person visits. What these issues are, and the format used to collect them, will evolve over a period of months as the intact work group begins to "flesh out" its daily meeting and primary visual display content and procedures.

KCG 20 Keys Assessment and Long-Term Improvement Plan

Definition—The last element of the lean daily management system is the KCG 20 Keys assessment and long-term improvement action plan. Each work group, from Engineering to Customer Service, has its own KCG 20 Keys action plan that outlines the steps required to move upward on a predetermined scale toward world class. Due to the critical nature of this tool and its central position within Office Kaizen, a detailed explanation of the purpose and operation of the KCG 20 Keys is presented separately in chapter 9.

8

Mentoring and Training

"The LDMS is the missing piece," George said aloud. "It's important that big changes run well, but most problems are caused by accumulations of surface waste in everyday work. The LDMS attacks all of these wastes all of the time. We're going to do Office Kaizen, and we're going to do it right. I think we have an opportunity to take a giant step and I'm going to do everything I can to make sure we don't trip."

George called his leadership team together once again: "Office Kaizen is our future, and SLIM-IT is the tool that will make it possible," announced George proudly. He hadn't even read the entire book but he knew it was the answer. He knew he had to take a bold step to show them that things were different. If he couldn't take a chance, who could? He saw the executives nodding their heads in tandem. He knew they were wondering how long the program would last. George pulled a box of books onto the table and began to hand them out. He said, "I've got a little something for you to read over the weekend. We're going to get together on Monday and talk about how to make this work."

Mentoring is vital to those who move forward with Office Kaizen. Mentoring is the mechanism within SLIM-IT that shepherds, guides, and compels the success of an Office Kaizen implementation. It cannot be omitted or short-changed. Without an in-depth understanding of the requirements of mentoring and a plan to provide it for each site that pursues Office Kaizen, an implementation effort has only a one in 100 chance of succeeding (and any that do succeed will take three to five times longer than they would with mentoring support).

WHY IS MENTORING ESSENTIAL?

The organizational constraints and complications created by human motivation and group dynamics (discussed in chapter 5) must be dealt with proactively to successfully implement anything. The leadership wastes that routinely sabotage management initiatives must be dramatically reduced if any change is to be sustained. Through mentoring, SLIM-IT turns these negative inherent tendencies into positive forces for sustained change.

Mentoring is real-time, omnipresent teaching, coaching, and guiding of every element of the SLIM-IT model as Office Kaizen is implemented. It is on-the-job, person-to-person, person-to-group feedback, coaching, and advice to the executive steering committee (ESC), champions, team leaders, change teams, and intact work groups by people who are skilled in Office Kaizen, SLIM-IT, related tools, and in working with people in a coaching role.

The mentor must be involved in the ESC meetings, and they must be viewed and treated as having equal stature to the other attendees. They must be free (indeed, required) to strongly facilitate, correct, and guide the meeting. The mentor must also provide feedback to individuals after the meeting, if required (for example, "Jeffrey, it might be a good idea if you let the other ESC members do more of the talking. You already know the answers, but they have to get there by working it out."). The mentor must also provide the same support for the change team leaders, change team members, and intact work groups as they install the lean daily management system (LDMS).

A mentor must:

1. Be a self-assured individual who can hold their own in front of both management and employee groups.

2. Be older rather than younger. (There is almost no chance that a group of more mature managers and executives is going to take candid feedback about management style and behavior from a 25-year-old, no matter how sharp they are.)

3. Possess a strong personality (in order to survive the abuse and frustration).

4. Be on the ESC as a formal, recognized member (appointed after selection as the mentor).

5. Possess knowledge of Office Kaizen and SLIM-IT methods and have some experience applying them.

6. Be able to teach (person-to-person) at all levels of the organization.

7. Be discreet about confidences.

8. Understand how organizations work and have the patience to use personal means of influence before "running to the ESC and champions" whenever there is a problem.

9. Be results oriented.

10. Be committed full-time as a mentor in all but the smallest implementation efforts.

11. Be viewed as having "personal power." (It is important for status purposes that the mentor is viewed as having influence as an individual, as a member of the ESC, and as an Office Kaizen expert. While this characteristic is related to the others above, it is also an intangible that might not be present in sufficient quantity, even if most of the other characteristics are present.)

As you can see, the mentor must be a very formidable person. Managers, when asked to suggest a candidate from their area, cannot always be trusted to make sacrifices for the sake of the organization as a whole. Usually, the people who are first suggested are the "walking wounded" who will not be missed. Such people are not mentoring material. If the mention of an individual as a candidate mentor elicits expressions such as "My department can't function without her," "He's critical to day-to-day operations," or "You're taking my best person," it is a fair bet that the individual is an excellent mentor candidate. An added bonus is that "taking" the candidate from the manager will force the manager to develop other resources rather than rely on the same superstar all of the time.

HOW MANY MENTORS?

Every organization is different, and every site in an organization is unique. Some sites are resistant to change, and some have more or less enthusiastic and skilled management teams than others. Yet, within a small range of variation, the number of mentors required to implement Office Kaizen is dependent primarily upon the size of the site (in terms of the number of personnel who work there). It might seem that the number of required mentors would be driven to a large extent by the leadership team's desire to proceed slower or faster than "normal." Strangely, this is not true. In fact, there is only one speed at which Office Kaizen can be safely implemented anywhere. It is akin to growing a tree. Given too much or too little sun, fertilizer, or water, a specific tree will suffer and not grow at an optimum rate for long-term health. Provided the optimum amount of nutrients and sunlight, the tree will grow as efficiently as possible.

Implementing a large-scale change such as Office Kaizen is the same type of process. If the implementation goes too slow, either by intention or because of difficulties, the initiative is in great danger. In slower than benchmark implementations, bottom-line results are hard to notice (because most of the organization is not involved). This puts the leadership team and the mentors in the position of defending an effort whose benefits are difficult to detail to other managers and corporate personnel who may be skeptical or outright opponents. A slow implementation generates very little excitement, and the leadership team will become frustrated and bored ("We have to do this for years?!" and "Why do we have to have these meetings every week? There's hardly anything happening."). If only a part of the site is implementing Office Kaizen, the personnel from that area will receive mixed and counterproductive messages from employees from other areas. Going too fast is not an option either. Change takes time and cannot go faster than its internal speed limit. People and groups need soaking time to absorb and adopt new behaviors.

Managers and supervisors that are not involved can feel left out or lucky and the ones that are forced to participate may feel victimized (or lucky). Perhaps most critically, in order to change the behaviors of a group of people, it is necessary for desired actions of many individuals to be reinforced at every possible occasion. This helps to create new norms of behavior more quickly.

The estimates of numbers of mentors and implementation durations given in the following sections are based on the optimum that generally applies.

It is essential to provide a range of mentoring skills to a site. If every mentor were to be a world-class, experienced expert, many of them would not have enough to do in order to keep them challenged. Not only would the site be paying for skills they could not apply (you cannot exceed the internal speed limit of the site), the experts would be bored and the effort would suffer. If the mentors were all rookies without skills, the implementation would fail for obvious reasons. With a variety of mentor skill levels, experts play the lead role and teach the rookies (who are future leaders). The lower skill levels are constantly learning and being challenged as they manage smaller pieces of the effort and the experts have a broad mix of coaching, teaching, and staff development activities to keep them excited (and developing into the site's "super-leaders" of the future). A rough standard of mentoring expertise might be:

Expert   Adept at dealing with people at all levels, experienced and knowledgeable in all facets of Office Kaizen, SLIM-IT, reengineering, and problem-solving tools. Can teach and coach at any level and is a true leader waiting for their chance to excel.

Skilled   Knows how to deal with people well, is at least familiar with Office Kaizen and SLIM-IT concepts, is experienced in applying many reengineering and problem-solving tools, and can teach and coach at most levels in the organization. These are future leaders who need a little more hand-to-hand experience in Office Kaizen.

Technician Can deal with most people fairly well and is well skilled and experienced in applying several reengineering tools.

Rookie   Seems to like people, can take abuse, is a hard worker, is willing to learn by starting at the bottom, and has a positive attitude.

Table 8.1 provides information concerning required numbers of mentors and implementation durations for sites with various numbers of personnel. For each site size, two rows of data are provided. The upper row, labeled "Initial Stage," presents the number of mentors required to get the SLIM-IT scramjet designed, built, ignited, and powering-up at a site. SLIM-IT mechanisms are in place and being used with some facility: the ESC is established; all change efforts have formal teams with champions, team leaders, charters, and teams; there are regular kaizen blitzes; and every intact work group has a fully installed LDMS.

The second row for each site size is labeled "Under Way." This row shows the number of mentors needed to take SLIM-IT from "Initial Stage" to operating at full power long enough to create a completely new, self-sustaining culture. At the point of reaching the end of the time periods cited for the "Under Way" levels, Office Kaizen would be immune from all but the most disastrous consequences. The far right hand column presents the approximate number of months required to achieve the "Initial Stage" (top row of each site size) and "Under Way" (bottom row of each site size) stages of SLIM-IT.

For example, Table 8.1 shows that a site with 1000 employees would require one expert mentor, one skilled mentor, one technician mentor, and one rookie mentor (a total of four people) for 12 months (months one to 12 of the implementation effort) to attain "Initial Stage" status. The bottom row of the 1000 employees section specifies that a lower level of mentoring support would be required for months 13 through 42 in order to move from "Initial Stage" status to "Under Way" status. The lower level of mentoring support for months 13 through 42 is displayed as one expert mentor, one skilled mentor, and one rookie mentor, for a total of three people.

Table 8.1   Numbers of mentors of various skill/experience levels required to implement Office Kaizen.

Number of Site Personnel	Implementation Level	Mentor Type				Total Personnel	Duration in Months
		Expert	Skilled	Technician	Rookie		
6000	Initial Stage	3	6	8	8	25	1–22
	Under Way	1	2	2	3	8	23–48
5000	Initial Stage	2	5	6	8	21	1–20
	Under Way	1	2	2	2	7	21–48
4000	Initial Stage	2	4	4	6	16	1–18
	Under Way	1	1	2	2	6	19–44
3000	Initial Stage	2	3	3	5	13	1–16
	Under Way	1	1	1	2	5	17–44
2000	Initial Stage	2	2	2	2	8	1–14
	Under Way	1	1	1	1	4	15–42
1000	Initial Stage	1	1	1	1	4	1–12
	Under Way	1	1		1	3	13–42
750	Initial Stage	1	1		1	3	1–10
	Under Way	1			1	2	10–38
500	Initial Stage	1	1		1	3	1–8
	Under Way	1			1	2	9–32
250	Initial Stage	1		1		2	1–6
	Under Way	1				1	7–24
100	Initial Stage	1				1	1–4
	Under Way		1			1	5–18

As a site transitions from "Initial Stage" status to moving through the "Under Way" development period, the lower number of required mentors provides a golden opportunity to move a mentor or two into a line management position. After all, who would be a better proponent of the Office Kaizen management style? This then permits rookie mentors to move into technician mentor spots (assuming that they have earned the right) and so on. In this way, the implementation effort becomes a feeder to the management recruitment/development process. Indeed, the mentoring process can be thought of as a Navy Seal management boot camp for the future leaders of the site (and the larger organization, if there is one).

At first glance, the number of mentors may seem high. It is not. In fact, Office Kaizen implementations almost always quickly produce a net gain in value-added resources available to a site. When an ESC is established and begins to take inventory of and evaluate the change initiatives that are ongoing, tremendous waste is always discovered that can be applied to Office Kaizen implementation duties.

Although it is frightening to encounter firsthand (if you are a site or higher level executive), there are always significant resources being devoted to dead ends that nobody has "had the heart" to kill off (assuming that they know about it). The people working on these hidden projects may be hard at work but they are revving their engines with absolutely no connection to a transmission of any sort. Other important initiatives launched by single departments have been floundering for months, eating up time and money, but getting no support because other areas do not know or care what they are doing. A few critical initiatives are found to be moving as slow as molasses running uphill in an Artic winter because they are not being properly supported or staffed. At the same time, management may think things are progressing but is invariably shocked (shocked!) when the next irregularly held briefing demonstrates that the effort is dead in the water. Resources will then be stripped from other efforts (that will then suffer) in a fire drill to save the day.

When the deadwood efforts are eliminated, when the vital efforts are properly staffed and championed, almost every site finds that it can get its work done and provide the resources to mentor the Office Kaizen effort with no staff count additions. There will be complaining, of course (for example, the ubiquitous "Our plates are already full!"), but such resistance is normal, to be expected, and is ignored by a wise leader who understands organizations. Additional benefits accrue from fewer future problems of the same type, faster implementations of any new changes, and the continuous improvement that is produced by the LDMS in every intact work group.

However, even in the most rare case in which the implementation resources could not be rounded up via repair and rationalization of current initiatives, what price is too high to pay for a strategic competitive advantage? The general ratio of mentors to personnel across the various site sizes is about one to 250. New technologies and innovations (for example, the development of new products and services, EIS software systems, and the like) require far more implementation resources (not to mention capital expenditures), are inherently more risky, and deliver only short-term competitive advantages (if any). You never get something valuable for nothing. Office Kaizen is a tremendous value; it provides a long-term, self-sustaining, continuously increasing strategic competitive advantage. However, it must be mentored into place. Mentoring can be had at a bargain price (compared to high-tech innovations) but that price must be paid.

WHAT MUST BE MENTORED?

The following are many (but not all) of the topics, processes, activities, and concepts that must be mentored. Keep in mind that mentoring means: teaching the basics (if required), demonstrating how to do it the first time, observing and coaching subsequent performance, and providing continuous feedback at first and then occasionally over time. This must be done every day to the site executive, the ESC members, champions, change team leaders, change team members, all meetings, middle management and supervisors that interact with the change teams, and for intact work groups that are implementing the LDMS. Some of the topics/concepts/tools/skills are:

- Formation/selection of the ESC

- Meeting management and coaching of the ESC meetings

- Identification of all current change initiatives

- Customization of the Office Kaizen implementation to incorporate and integrate essential current programs, jargon, and company culture

- Generation of preliminary charters for current change initiatives

- Coaching of ESC on preliminary charter structure and development for each change team

- Coaching of ESC charter negotiation with change teams

- Selection of a champion for each current change initiative

- Coaching of proper champion behavior

- Selection of a team leader for each current change initiative

- Coaching of proper team leader behavior
- Selection and formation of a team to take over each current change initiative
- Coaching of proper change team meeting management
- Coaching of charter structure and development for the team:
  - Brainstorming techniques
  - Schedule development
  - Deliverables development
  - RACI development (responsibility charting)
- Coaching of team members in working with various levels of the organization:
  - Supervisors
  - Intact work groups
  - Managers
  - Technical personnel
- Coaching of development of "as is" (current state) diagrams of current processes
- Coaching of development of "to be" (future state) diagrams of current processes (the above two items are elements of reengineering flowcharts)
- Coaching of project management with the change teams
- Schedule maintenance/attainment
  - Cost/benefit tracking
  - Metric development
  - Communications with the organization
  - Development/assurance of ongoing support mechanisms
- Coaching of installation of the LDMS into each intact work group:
  - Primary visual display (PVD)
  - Daily work group meetings
  - Kaizen action sheet system

- KCG 20 Keys
- Short-interval leadership
- Metrics generation and tracking
- Office Kaizen/reengineering blitzes
- Planning
- Coaching of a blitz week
- Follow-up ("sweep" week)
- Development of an Office Kaizen implementation plan
- DILO (day-in-the-life-of) analysis
- The "5S" method in general
- Structured problem solving
- The seven quality control tools:
  - Run charts
  - Simple flowcharting
  - Histograms
  - Pareto charts
  - Cause-and-effect diagrams
  - Scatter plots
  - SPC charts:
    - Variable charts
    - Attribute charts
- Workplace organization (signs, labels, and so on)
- Work flow balancing and leveling (site and work group)
- Kanban placement and design (in high-volume environments such as insurance, bank back office, and so on)
- Cell layout and design
- Skill versatility matrices
- Exposition participation/feedback

- Financial analysis (for cost/return studies)

- Error-proofing approaches

Every organization can identify many of the above items as tools, approaches, and methods they have used and/or are currently using. The utility of mentoring (and of SLIM-IT in general) is that it assures that only the proper and most appropriate methods are applied when they are required (with appropriate follow-through). Regrettably, many organizations are victimized severely by "hammeritis" ("If all you have is a hammer, everything starts to look like a nail"), in which tools are applied because the "expert" needs to find an application for what they know. Mentors who are knowledgeable and experienced are able to draw from the above (and other methods such as value stream mapping) to determine what is the best tool or method for each situation (all within the framework of Office Kaizen).

THE PLACE OF TRAINING IN OFFICE KAIZEN

The extensive list of necessary mentor skill and knowledge demonstrates that a great deal of training must be provided to mentors (site coaches/coordinators) if Office Kaizen is to succeed. Mentor training must be provided in real time, on the job, so that skills are applied and practical; if the mentor cannot learn to handle the messy, chaotic stream of events in a typical organization, they will be only marginally successful. Therefore, mentors must be coached by a master practitioner who has "seen it all" and "done it all" (often described with the Japanese term for master teacher: *sensei*). This training is best provided by having the mentors attend a rigorous six- to 10-week (or more) training program in which they learn, do, coach, and mentor all of the above-listed methods/tools in operating work areas (often rotating among several sites with different "problems").

The type of training that must be provided for other personnel also differs from that provided by the traditional training programs of the past. It is pointless to train large numbers of employees and managers in narrow technical skills (such as statistical process control or even problem-solving methods) if they are not going to be required to use them in a structured manner soon after the training is delivered. Office Kaizen provides a structure (of change teams and intact work groups) that will "point" to the people and areas that require training when and if it is appropriate. Therefore, as with mentors, most people in most sites should learn tools and techniques as they use them.

For example, instead of teaching value stream analysis in a classroom, employees should learn it by being part of a change team and/or by participating in a blitz event that uses it (or by being briefed by a team that has used it in their area). No money or time is wasted on training that won't be used or on training that will be forgotten by the time it is needed. Some would say that this approach leaves a number of employees in the dark regarding some tools and techniques. True, but that's life. Other people can explain it to them (none of this is rocket science) and they will learn soon enough by using it themselves as opportunities to participate on change teams and blitz teams present themselves.

Nonetheless, a small amount of introductory training is essential for the management team at each site (down to and including middle management). The ESC and middle management of a site must be shown the basic "what it is" and "how it works" elements of Office Kaizen; they must understand the big picture and what will be happening at their site. This can easily be accomplished in a tightly structured, two-day workshop that covers the contents and concerns of this book. Of course, each member of this group must also participate as a full-time worker-bee in at least one blitz event as soon as possible.

IMPLEMENTATION ALTERNATIVES

There are seven basic approaches that organizations have used in the past for implementing large-scale initiatives such as EIS systems, wide-ranging reengineering efforts, corporate "shake-ups," and so forth. The same seven approaches will probably be considered as possible methods for providing the mentoring element of SLIM-IT. The following sections briefly discuss the suitability of each of these alternatives for supporting the implementation of Office Kaizen.

1. *An earnest attempt by site management.* In this approach, the leadership team holds its first ESC meeting and gets started. This sounds like the ideal approach, because it is essential for site leadership to participate actively. When the existing management team mentors the organization without any outside help, it sets a tremendous leadership example. Unfortunately, even though this is the ideal approach in theory, it rarely works. Only one management team in 5000 has the proper combination of knowledge, skill, time, and courage to mentor themselves and their organization and lead the implementation of the LDMS and blitz events. When this approach is attempted, the initiative usually dies after six months, at which time victory is declared and the next "program" is launched.

2. *Site management "decree."* This is the all-too-common, "send out the memo" implementation approach that has killed countless thousands of initiatives. Management describes its existing activities as fulfilling all of the executive steering committee roles and instructs department managers to implement the LDMS. There is a flurry of random and damaging activity for six to nine months until everyone figures out that management has lost interest.

3. *Existing site trainers.* Most sites have a skills trainer and/or management-quality trainer (or several of them). Shortsighted leaders see Office Kaizen as just another tool and assume that the usual training crew can handle it. Few trainers and content experts have the broad management background, leadership capabilities, and management skills necessary to be mentors at the higher levels of the organization. In addition, they rarely have the personal influence and confidence (not to mention permission) to deal with the management team in a forthright and firm manner. This approach disintegrates into a tools program after three to nine months as every mentor suggestion is rebuffed by resistant managers. The result is a few small pockets of good efforts adrift on a vast sea of neglect and disinterest.

4. *Site mentors are selected and "learn-as-you-go."* Enthusiastic people of good character are selected as mentors and told to read a few books, get a little training, and get started. This is the same situation as scenario two above, with even less background in tools and methods. Selection of good people usually nets a group that is very enthusiastic at first. When they run into the usual resistance, management meddling, and lack of leadership, they fall apart more quickly than trainers (trainers face these problems with every initiative they lead and are thus steeled to deal with indifference). This type of effort usually dies very quickly, leaving behind all sorts of ill feelings on the part of the mentors.

5. *Corporate "assistance."* The Chinese have an old saying (that they still employ and that is still valid): "The mountains are high and the Emperor/Communist Party headquarters is far away." In other words, if the folks at corporate aren't bothering you, don't invite them to. Sending out the invitation is fraught with danger. The problem is that few central office personnel have the skills and background to provide meaningful Office Kaizen support (where would they have learned it in a traditional organization?). The "help" will most likely consist of a few blitzes and/or classroom training in either philosophy or isolated tools. This is worse than nothing. The training will not include the critical structure of SLIM-IT and even if they cover it, they will not be around day-to-day to provide the

critical mentoring. The danger, aside from the waste of time and resources, presents itself in several ways: 1) once begun, it is almost impossible to stop the "help" when it becomes apparent it is not working, 2) the helpers will generate a need for regular "status reports" which will grow in size and complexity, and 3) the site will be discouraged (or forbidden) from obtaining additional help because it "conflicts" with "our approach." The effort usually dies in six months to a year, often with concurrent replacement of site executives, because they "did not get the job done."

6. *External resources implement Office Kaizen ("while management does its regular job").* This is the manner in which many organizations use consultants. The primary problem is that the site leadership team has no ownership of the implementation and is not forced to develop the skill and knowledge base necessary to sustain Office Kaizen once the consultants leave. It is much like the difference between reading a number of books about heart surgery and the related anatomy and watching an operation and actually performing the operation itself. The eye–hand, cognitive feedback loop that is essential to a skilled, successful surgeon can only be learned through repeated, daily, mentored practice. Another problem is that if the consultants do all of the implementation, there will be minimum customization of the consultant's standard approach to incorporate the specific and unique needs of the site. These types of efforts work well initially and are very popular with site leadership teams (because site leaders don't have to do anything different). The efforts almost always (90 percent of the time) fall apart within a year after the consultants leave, because daily leadership miscues and lack of attention send contrary signals and gradually pour sand into the gears. A year later, little is left but pockets of excellence being sustained by a few determined individual supervisors and managers.

7. *External resources "mentor the mentors and management."* This approach balances the best of the "leaders do it themselves" method with the reality of organizations and the availability of special skills and experience in the form of consultants. Right from the start, the existing site management team is required to perform all of the SLIM-IT tasks. They are mentored on a daily basis by the consultants. At the same time, the consultants help select and train an exceptional site employee(s) to be mentor(s). This training is done in real time, on the job. By the time the implementation is "up and running," the site has an experienced management team that has been "doing Office Kaizen," and a team of experienced, in-the-trenches mentors who already have the trust of the organization, are experienced, and can take over. If they are allowed to do their jobs (no reassignments and dramatic management leadership changes for two years), this approach is about as error-proof as a human endeavor can be.

Mentoring is not an easy task, but if it is done correctly, it will return the time and effort on the bottom line tenfold over the following few years and one hundredfold over the next decade. The mission of a site leader or an executive with multi-site responsibilities is to assure that sites get the mentoring they need, not just "eyewash." There is always tremendous pressure to do less, because effective mentors make changes that are painful. Real leaders make reassuring comments to the inevitable complaints but compel people to do the right thing.

9

The KCG 20 Keys Approach

Some of George's leadership team had congregated to discuss their boss's latest idea. "Thank God we aren't going to try to do this on our own! These are not simple changes in procedures," exclaimed the VP of Corporate Initiatives, skimming the chapter on mentoring. "Office Kaizen promises big results. It claims to change everybody's expectations and behaviors," said the VP of Administration. "Well, I hope so, because when it comes to 'trying new things,' my team has about as much enthusiasm as a teenager digging ditches in July," added the VP of Human Resources.

Meanwhile, George was plagued by a nagging concern. He had noticed in the past that the initial enthusiasm for many programs died after a few initial successes. He remembered the customer satisfaction push of several years back. As soon as the survey results showed that Biginslow was above the industry median, enthusiasm flagged. "Everybody, managers and hands-on workers, began to feel we were good enough," thought George. "As a result, focus dissolved, discipline eroded, and the effort died. What does Office Kaizen do to avoid this trap?"

There is nothing new about the concept of identifying "*X*" number of important factors and then measuring how a person or group performs against them. However, several important characteristics differentiate the KCG 20 Keys approach from more typical "*X* things to get better on" approaches. In fact, the long-term success of Office Kaizen depends upon these differences.

Let us assume that you are a year or two into your Office Kaizen effort and things are going well. SLIM-IT is up and running and the lean daily management system (LDMS) is installed in every intact work group. All change initiatives are working under the ESC–champions–charter–change team structure. You can feel the energy and see the results on the bottom line. Many nagging problems have gone away, visitors are impressed with how things look and operate, and there are fewer internal and external customer complaints. Management finally has time to think about future innovations for more than five minutes at a time. Things couldn't be better, right? As you might expect, it is not that easy, even with Office Kaizen.

Almost without exception, first as barely heard whispers and eventually in semi-defiant tones, you will encounter a type of resistance that you never imagined. You will hear, "Why should we have to keep getting better? We're already world class. What's the sense in pushing so hard?" The organization will have come so far so quickly that many people will have no reason to believe more is necessary or even possible. After a period of significant improvement, they will be tempted to believe the organization is world class when, in actuality, it is only operating at a level of fair to good compared to others in the industry.

This distorted view is a hurdle that must be cleared in every world-class race. You can delay it somewhat by constantly communicating competitors' costs, prices, and market pressures through every communication channel possible. Charts posted on the primary visual display (PVD) with occasional review in the daily work group meeting will help, but the complaints will eventually arrive. It is natural for employees to believe that management wants to "squeeze them" as much as possible. It takes more than a year or two of Office Kaizen to completely erase the decades-old heritage of traditional leadership.

The KCG 20 Keys approach propels the SLIM-IT implementation over this hurdle before it presents itself. Almost right from the start, the KCG 20 Keys establish a set of world-class benchmarks, performance expectations, and a roadmap for improvement within each intact work group. The KCG 20 Keys show each work group exactly where it stands vis-à-vis world class, while providing a consistent methodology across all intact work groups and allowing for customization to unique work situations and functions.

It seems as if every time an initiative or program washes up onto an organization's beach and then returns to the misbegotten, black depths from whence it came, it leaves behind a reporting requirement. The program becomes a "zombie"; its soul is dead, but the hideous, undead reporting requirement lurches to and fro amidst the cubicles of the organization, leaving behind a noxious slime of surface waste. Everyone knows the zombie is lifeless inside; but they are afraid to challenge it—they don't know who, if anyone, controls it. Nobody needs more of this. The KCG 20 Keys approach does not assess results. Instead, it allows an intact work group to determine how well it is *implementing the processes* of Office Kaizen. Results are important but most organizations already have sufficient reporting requirements for results to last 1000 years. We will discuss the Office Kaizen approach to metrics in chapter 11.

The distinction between measuring results and assessing process implementation progress is critical. An illustrative example relates to golf. If a golfer wishes to improve his tee shots, he measures progress by keeping a detailed record of drive distances and attempting to figure out what creates the longer drives. Is it stance, weather, mood, energy, diet, amount of sleep, and so on? If the golfer happens to be using a different brand of balls during a particular run of good tee shots, he may conclude that the ball caused the improvement and switch brands. As many golfers can attest, ball type alone rarely yields significant improvements. Managers often make the same mistake with performance metrics: they assume that whatever produced good results once will work again. The difficulty is that most influences on complex processes are unknown, external, hidden, confounded with other causes, or random. Thus, the cause that gets the credit for the improvement is whatever is noticed. The true cause is most often never recognized.

Faced with this complex situation, the default position of most managers is to assume that "good management" causes good results. Thus, a period of good results is usually followed by higher-level managers exhorting lower-level managers to "keep doing what you were doing but give me five percent more next year." Since the lower-level managers are not generally applying a consistent management philosophy and/or tactics (focus and structure), their efforts produce wild swings in performance caused by unknown influences. Many golfers experience this same phenomenon.

A much more effective method for a golfer who wishes to improve is to hire a golf pro to analyze their drives (and general stance) and then coach the golfer through several rounds to develop a structured, disciplined approach. A good pro does not focus on distance but instead instructs the student on the process of perfecting the individual components of a world-class golf shot—"Develop good form and habits and the distance will come." This is the mission of the KCG 20 Keys approach. Each key is built upon the Office Kaizen philosophy. Each individual work group focuses on a limited range of consistent, world-class options as to *how* it must "swing from the tee" toward the "Office Kaizen green" of world-class performance.

For example, one of the KCG 20 Keys of Office Kaizen is primary visual display (PVD). In order to progress to level two (of five) on this key, a work group must have a PVD with information that is up-to-date 80 percent of the time (four days out of five). To attain level four, the PVD must be 99 percent accurate and timely (only one miss every few months) and work group members must be responsible for most PVD maintenance. If all intact work groups in a site are using such a PVD in their daily work group meeting, massive amounts of surface waste will fall before the sword (or driver) of Office Kaizen. It happens without fail, no matter how results are measured—the right process always produces the right results. Over time, this creates a strategic competitive advantage, just as the same attention to processes rather than results knocks three to 10 strokes off an average golfer's handicap.

There are many versions of the KCG 20 Keys. Different versions are appropriate for intact work groups in different functional areas. There are versions for work groups in customer service, human resources, sales, marketing, manufacturing, and product development, just to mention a few. As the name implies, the KCG 20 Keys of Office Kaizen is the set that is applicable to any general intact work group in an office setting. This set of keys, shown in Figure 9.1, presents 20 factors that are critical to the enduring success of an Office Kaizen effort.

1. Leadership	11. Daily Work Group Meetings
2. Documentation Management	12. Problem Solving
	13. Internal Customer Service
3. Deadlines & Commitments	14. Priority Management
4. Competence	15. Work Standards
5. Time Management	16. Primary Visual Display
6. Workplace Arrangement	17. Time Control and Commitment
7. Skill Flexibility	
8. Roles and Responsibilities	18. Metrics & Measurements
9. Ownership of Objectives	19. Budget and Costs
10. Cleaning and Organizing	20. External Customer Service

Figure 9.1 The 20 key categories of the KCG 20 Keys of Office Kaizen.

If a specific key does not apply to a situation, it can be replaced with a newly devised key. If possible, it is best to use the set in Figure 9.1 (shown in full detail in appendix A) for at least six months before changes are made. At that point, the minor "wordsmithing" that once seemed important is usually deemed unnecessary.

Each key has five levels of performance, from one (lowest) to five (best). Performance on a key is never less than one; every work group starts with an assumed score of 20. There are no half points or fractional values. If every stated element of a level is not attained, the key is assessed at the next lowest level. This short-circuits the gamesmanship of fractional values. The maximum possible score of 100 on any set is all but impossible to reach. The highest score I have ever encountered face-to-face from an intact work group or team was 67. A unique one- to three-sentence description describes each level of each key.

Table 9.1 presents the general guidelines that are used to construct the detailed definitions for the levels of each key.

The rating scale guidelines shown in Table 9.1 are designed to fulfill several purposes:

1. Every work group starts with 20 points. This helps avoid the defeatism that a score of two or five out of 100 would generate.

2. The definitions of the levels are designed to produce a starting score between 25 and 35 for an intact work group that is doing a decent job in a traditionally-run organization. If an intact work group scores above 35, it is an indication of a well-run work group. Scores above 45 either indicate an exceptional group (for a traditionally-run organization) or the need for a validation audit on the part of the KCG 20 Keys implementation team.

3. It is relatively easy to move from level one to level two. It is harder to move to level three and very, very difficult to progress to level four. Level five is almost impossible to attain on more than a few keys (over a period of a few years). The designed-in ease of picking up points in the first year or two is critical. It builds a group's confidence so that when the going gets tougher downstream, the group will believe it can do anything.

If we were to use the above guidelines to develop a set of KCG 20 Keys for an individual's golf game (developing keys for an individual is tricky and not straightforward; we will discuss it later in this chapter), key one might be "Driving from the tee." Table 9.2 displays a version of the five levels of this key.

Table 9.1 General guidelines for the development of detailed key levels.

Level	Qualitative Definition	General Qualitative Characteristic
One	Traditional	The usual mess; reactive, few, or bad systems; many problems; "Oh, well . . ."
Two	Learning	Awareness established; first small steps taken
Three	Leading	Occasional glitches, sometimes serious
Four	World class	Outstanding; not quite always automatic
Five	Currently invincible	Seamless, transparent, automatic excellence

Table 9.2 The five levels of the "Driving from the Tee" key.

Level	Qualitative Definition	General Qualitative Characteristic	Version-Specific Qualitative Characteristic
One	Traditional	The usual mess; reactive, few, or bad systems; many problems; "Oh, well . . ."	Position of head, arms, grip, legs, and shoulders varies wildly; swing is choppy and not consistent.
Two	Learning	Awareness established; first small steps taken	Standard grip established; approach stance consistent (70% of the time); head and shoulders kept in line most of the time (80%).
Three	Leading	Frequent glitches, sometimes serious	Stance, grip, and body orientation are well maintained through swing (90%); backswing is consistent most of the time (70%).
Four	World class	Outstanding; not quite always automatic	Stance, grip, and body orientation are maintained through swing; backswing is consistent 95% of the time.
Five	Currently invincible	Seamless, transparent, automatic excellence	There is less than 1% deviation from consistent textbook positioning.

Most average golfers would be ecstatic to attain level three as shown in Table 9.2. This is as it should be; level three is at the "leading" level and represents superior performance compared to average golfers, but it is far away from "world class" and "currently invincible." The KCG 20 Keys approach does not grade on a curve. The top 10 golf professionals would probably rate fours ("world class") most of the time. On good days, these same pros might attain level five ("currently invincible").

This structure, with level five representing the best of the best, is the mechanism that keeps work groups honest. They may think they are doing great, but their own set of keys will not allow them to fool themselves. Strangely enough, once involved with Office Kaizen, work groups are brutally frank about everything. They don't mind being honest about their performance, because they know they can only improve on the items they can control. Office Kaizen places the responsibility of implementing the lean daily management system on each intact work group (with management support and mentoring, of course). Since they possess a significant level of control, they are willing and eager to work hard for their own satisfaction (and recognition from the larger organization). Implementation of the KCG 20 Keys is fairly straightforward. Success with the KCG 20 Keys is dependent on the visual display of the graph that will be posted on the group's PVD. Thus, it is foolish to introduce the KCG 20 Keys into an intact work group until a PVD is established and being used in a well-run, daily work group meeting.

The general procedures for implementing and sustaining the KCG 20 Keys in all the intact work groups at a site are:

1. A change team reporting to the ESC determines in general what versions of the KCG 20 Keys will be used in various groups and gets approval from the ESC.

2. The same change team designs an implementation plan (that is, who will introduce the work group leaders to the approach, what will the standard KCG 20 Keys graph look like, how will required modifications to key versions be handled and approved, and so on).

3. The ESC determines what the total point goal is for three to four years in the future. Each intact work group has the same goal (a four-year goal of 70 points is most typical).

4. The change team trains the intact work group leaders (what the KCG 20 Keys are, how they work, and so on).

5. Each intact work group leader introduces the approach to their work group.

6. Each intact work group rates its current level of achievement.

7. Each intact work group calculates its annual point objective (for example, 70 – 30, the current score, = 40, which, divided by 4 years, results in a required goal of 10 points per year over the next four years).

8. Each intact work group selects the keys and points to work on during the next year.

9. Each intact work group selects the first key to work on during the next several weeks to a month (depending on current score and targets set by the site leader).

10. Each intact work group, led by the group leader, develops a plan for going after the first point on the first key it has selected.

11. As each point is achieved, the KCG 20 Keys graph posted on the PVD is changed and the next plan to earn the next point is generated, posted, and implemented.

12. The KCG 20 Keys implementation team and/or the site management team conducts "official" audits every six months. This is not mandatory, but it is an excellent way to provide positive attention to intact work groups that have done well (and provide an impetus for improvement for those that have not done enough).

13. At the end of the year, a formal audit is conducted (see step 11) and steps seven through 11 are repeated for the next year.

Steps five and six require a little more detail. It is best if the person viewed as the day-to-day leader introduces the KCG 20 Keys approach to the work group. In this meeting, each group member is given a set of the detailed level descriptions of the appropriate key version and a blank copy of the assessment graph (see appendix A for the KCG 20 Keys of Office Kaizen). The group leader explains the purpose of the keys (for example, benchmarking, self-assessment of the Office Kaizen implementation, or future improvement planning). The leader coaches the members through a group self-assessment. This is done one key at a time. Each member reads the key levels for the single key, and then the group discusses what the rating for the work group should be on that one key.

It is helpful if a large version of the graph is hand drawn on a white board or piece of paper so the group can all view the same display and perhaps see the range of opinions (if colored dots are used to denote each person's assessment). After the group has completed the rating of their current level of performance, they select keys for improvement over the next year and then prioritize the list. The group then develops a plan (which is posted on the PVD) for going after the first point level improvement. This step can be done in a second meeting later.

Figure 9.2 displays the graph of an intact work group's beginning self-assessment and its selected targets for the next year. The squares indicate the current or "as is" ratings. This initial assessment generated a fairly typical beginning score of 30 points for the group. The triangles represent

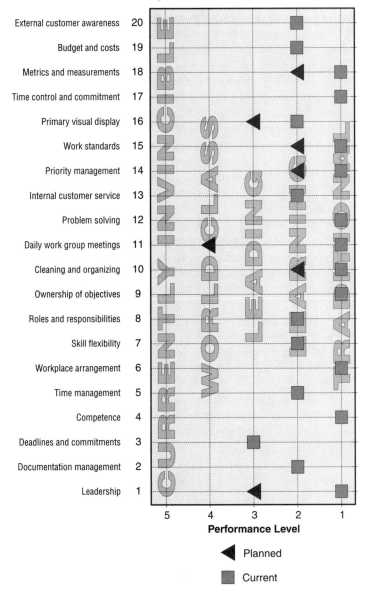

Figure 9.2　An intact work group's self-assessment and annual goals.

the improvement goals selected by the group that it will work on during the next year. It is not uncommon for a work group to obtain eight to 12 targeted points in the first year, plus an additional three to five that "just happen." This is because the keys are not orthogonal; that is, they do overlap. When enough improvement is going on, other areas are often "pulled along," even if they are not being specifically addressed.

The levels and keys selected by a particular intact work group may not be what the group manager, supervisor, or lead would have selected. It does not matter; the keys are all related and supportive. The more important consideration is that the group works together (belonging need satisfaction) to choose them (power and freedom need satisfaction). A well-respected group leader will have a lot of influence as he/she is helping the group assess and select keys. An intact work group leader without such influence should be grateful for any improvements he/she will get from whatever the group selects on its own.

Do not "stretch" the KCG 20 Keys beyond their design limits. Human beings require and benefit from positive interactions with others. A group's function in providing its members with belonging need satisfaction is a critical mechanism in the operation of the KCG 20 Keys approach. This influence is directly proportional to the size of the group (all other things being equal). As a group grows bigger than the 7±2 upper limit of effective intact work groups, the individuals begin to depend less on the group for satisfaction of their needs. They either locate another source of satisfaction outside the group or form a splinter, informal group within the larger group. Both of these consequences are damaging to what Office Kaizen is attempting to create.

Many organizations, attracted to the structure of approaches that look like the KCG 20 Keys, develop and apply a single set of keys to larger parts of an organization or an entire site. The site is evaluated as a whole (one score for the entire entity), and each area or department is then given a copy of the assessment and exhorted to "improve." This is not effective as a self-improvement and planning tool. Nobody feels responsible for results that are outside of their control; they only become frustrated. Any one person or small group rightly reasons, "I could kill myself to get here every day on time and tightly organize my work, but the department (or site) will still score a one on key 17 ("Time Control and Commitment") because others may not work as hard." This is why overarching site metrics never work well; they are little more than measurements. People feel little ownership about things they cannot control.

There are several additional mistakes that organizations make when applying approaches that look like the KCG 20 Keys, including:

1. *Applying the KCG 20 Keys to processes.* A process typically crosses many intact work groups. A single work group typically owns just a small part of it. If the process has problems, it should be addressed by a change team reporting to the ESC. This team may recommend some additional metrics for the process, but they must be tracked and action taken where appropriate (at the management level for innovations and within each of the intact work groups for process improvements).

2. *Applying the KCG 20 Keys to individuals.* It is the rare organization that does not look upon the power of the KCG 20 Keys and say, "We need the KCG 20 Keys of Leadership so that we can help our managers improve!" This can be done, but the pitfalls are not intuitively clear. It involves the principle of "actionality" that we will discuss in detail in chapter 11. The KCG 20 Keys approach works only at the level at which corrective actions can be taken by the group that is being assessed. It is also essential that the group can see the clear connection between its immediate efforts and increasing its KCG 20 Keys score.

For example, most attempts at sets of leadership keys include a "teamwork" key. This key assesses the area or department of the manager as to how well it operates in ad hoc groups to solve problems. At level three, the key for leadership teamwork might read, "Teams generally have defined objectives, tasks, and schedules . . ." Let's suppose the initial assessment is at level one ("little or no teamwork, and it is generally ineffective"). What can the manager do to correct the problem? Nothing, except perhaps provide coaching. The people that have to improve are not the ones being assessed. It is absolutely critical that the person or group assessed also be the person (or group) that has to make the changes. Intermediaries do not count. An acceptable teamwork key for an individual manager might read, at level three, "Actively reviews every formal team effort within the department once every week, with critical teams being coached more often during the week." This is something over which the manager has complete control and which measures an important element of their leadership behaviors (rather than results).

3. *Turning the KCG 20 Keys approach into a reporting requirement.* Do not waste time collecting key ratings and plans and reviewing them at a higher level. Instead, require site managers and their subordinates to assure that every work group is using the KCG 20 Keys. They should be walking around and observing, reading, and asking questions. If something is not right, they should be coaching the intact work group leader. The key is to manage the process, not endlessly dissect and react to meaningless, consolidated results.

4. *Computerizing the scoring and posting of results.* There are always individuals (at every level of every organization) who would rather sit in isolation and work on their computers than do value-added tasks. Once a blank copy of the KCG 20 Keys graph and a set of the detailed descriptions of the key levels have been printed, computers are no longer needed. Update charts with stickers, dots, and/or markers. The individual intact work groups should be able to maintain the information on the PVD without computer support for all data that is updated daily.

5. *Weighing the KCG 20 Keys.* These questions always arise: "Aren't some of the keys more important than others?" "Shouldn't we put them on the graph in order of importance (from key one to key 20)?" "Shouldn't we weigh the keys so some earn more points?" "Shouldn't we mandate action on the keys we think are important?" Some of the keys are probably more important, but who cares? It is more critical for the groups to take owner-ship than it is for management to be 100 percent correct. It is much more important to implement a 70 percent correct solution with 100 percent employee commitment than the other way around. Besides, as mentioned earlier, the keys are all interrelated, so the issue is more or less moot. Weighing the keys is a waste of time. It is usually too complicated to explain clearly and introduces endless opportunities for gamesmanship. Mandating action on certain keys short-circuits ownership by the intact work group. If the site needs widespread action on something, form a change team to attack it rather than trying to do it via the KCG 20 Keys.

FINAL COMMENT

The KCG 20 Keys approach does many good things. It keeps work groups honest about their current performance; tracks their goals and provides management with a means of setting high standards (for example, 70 points in all groups in four years); allows the work groups to take control of their own destiny; and does all of these with total group participation. While the groups are doing their day-to-day jobs, a small part of their efforts are directed toward continuous, long-term improvement. Over time, this creates a significant portion of the strategic competitive advantage that is the primary goal of Office Kaizen.

The most appealing aspect of the approach is that it allows each intact work group to "eat its own world-class elephant one bite at a time." When a traditional intact work group is functioning at the 25 to 35 point level (and is not familiar with the KCG 20 Keys), it is taken aback when shown the level three and four descriptions and told to "get there." It seems too much to expect, just like telling someone to eat an entire elephant. They don't know where to start or what to do so they give up. If, instead of discouraging them by displaying the whole elephant, they are shown a freezer filled with packages marked "elephant roasts, hot dogs, burgers, and stew meat" and are informed that their family (intact work group) must eat 500 pounds of elephant each year over the next four years, the task seems manageable; a few barbecues, some family dinners, a couple of parties, and most of the elephant is gone. The KCG 20 Keys approach allows each intact work group to eat its world-class elephant one bite at a time. A work group with a goal of earning 40 points over four years faces a long flight of stairs, not a seemingly impassable rock face.

10

How to Integrate Office Kaizen with "Big Name" Tools and Approaches

On Monday morning, the executive conference room of Biginslow buzzed with excitement about Office Kaizen. Playing devil's advocate, the VP of Finance asked, "What about all the other programs we have in the company? What do we do about them?" George jumped right in, "Look, let's make sure that we don't treat Office Kaizen like a flavor of the month, okay? It's a way of life, where the other 'programs' are just tools. Didn't you read chapter 10? Most of the tools we're using are fine for the purposes they were designed to fulfill. Unfortunately, in every case, we fell in love with the hope that each one would be our salvation, rather than an adjunct to our leadership. From now on, we lead with Office Kaizen and use the tools we need. Remember, Office Kaizen is a leadership method and management approach in which tools operate. You need both the leadership approach and the tools to get the job done."

In this chapter, a number of popular approaches and methodologies that are thought by many to function as significant mechanisms for improving competitiveness throughout an entire organization are examined. They are:

- Balanced scorecard
- Value stream mapping

- Reengineering/continuous improvement

- Six Sigma

- Lean manufacturing

- Project management

- ISO 9000/QS-9000

- DOE/Shainin

- Integrated product development

- Enterprise software

These approaches (and many others) can be of tremendous value in eliminating certain types of surface waste and energizing portions of an organization, sometimes to great competitive benefit. Elements of many of them are either directly incorporated into the structure of Office Kaizen or are utilized as important adjunct tools. However, while each of these approaches can be very powerful when accurately directed at specific issues, they are not capable of achieving a sustainable change in behavior and processes across a sufficiently comprehensive portion of the organization to create a competitive advantage over the long term.

This limitation is not a design flaw. The above approaches were designed to attain very specific objectives. A combination of business hype, "approach zealots," and the ever-present management quest for easy fixes to complex problems has created an environment in which almost any method with a catchy name is assigned an aura of "the complete answer" to almost any competitiveness problem. Even Office Kaizen will eventually be painted with this broad, ubiquitous brush if it attains general recognition. No single method or approach is (or has been or will be) a solution to every complex situation involving people and processes.

In those cases where the approaches discussed in this chapter are touted to be the primary driver to an organization's improved competitiveness, they have usually been supported by many other initiatives that were not as widely touted. For example, Six Sigma is almost automatically associated with the success of General Electric under the leadership of Jack Welch. While Six Sigma did many good things for GE, the organization also benefited from the vision and energy of Jack Welch, his personal involvement in teaching managers the "new way," lean manufacturing efforts that started years before Six Sigma arrived, design for manufacturability initiatives, outstanding leadership at lower levels, and exceptional strategic decision making and execution. To expect any method alone to do for other organizations what Six Sigma did for GE would be akin to expecting a high school baseball team to defeat the World Series champions, simply because they used the same brands of bats and gloves. When an organization is successful and a specific approach gets the credit, the recognized approach has always benefited from an environment in which leadership wastes had been under attack for some time by a variety of methods.

The core leadership issue thus becomes one of how to integrate approaches and methods rather than which single approach is best. Any successful drive toward competitiveness requires that leadership wastes be reduced at the same time that appropriate tools are used. There is only one truth here and it can be realized via an almost infinite combination of approaches and tools. The key issue is to integrate methods so that there is as little friction as possible and all key points are addressed. Office Kaizen without tools won't get the job done and any specific tool/approach won't realize even 10 percent of its potential if Office Kaizen (or something very much like it) is not used to address leadership wastes at all levels of the organization.

The following sections separately review major approaches and tools and how they can be integrated into Office Kaizen.

BALANCED SCORECARD

General Description—The balanced scorecard (BSC) was designed to enable managers to quickly appraise progress by evaluating a small to medium (five to 10 or so) number of key measures on a regular basis (daily to weekly to monthly). The primary purpose is to require executives or managers to focus on a variety of measures rather than one or two indicators (thus, the "balanced" aspect). An analogy with an aircraft or automotive control panel is often used to explain how the BSC operates: simply by scanning the instruments, the pilot can determine whether action needs to be taken. There is also an emphasis on indicators of results (for example, costs, profits, sales) rather than a check-off of individual tasks completed. This is because it is not uncommon to find that every single individual in a management team attained their objectives, yet the organization failed; the tasks were not sufficiently connected to bottom-line objectives. Over time, there has been a movement to push the balanced scorecard to lower-level managers, and sometimes to individual employees in the organization.

Strengths—The BSC is very effective at focusing the attention of upper management or any specific target group on a set of important measures. To the extent that consensus decision making is used to develop the balanced scorecard measures that the entire management team will support, this approach can be extremely effective. The proper set of metrics, driven from the head shed, can be invaluable in aligning the entire organization. Whether it's called a BSC or not, any leadership team that purports to be doing its job should have a limited set of measures that define what "good" is.

Best Integration Approach—While the BSC provides an organization's "pilots" with flight status, it assumes they know what to do when an indicator shows a problem. It is critical that upper management provide the organization with a uniform, consistent method for correcting the problem. For example, a world-class office environment has very fast cycle times for completing its work relative to average offices. If forced to react to a BSC with process cycle times (for the five most common tasks), a manager without Office Kaizen might sacrifice quality to achieve faster times. Office Kaizen would short-circuit this faulty approach. A BSC for a site or a facility must be developed by a change team reporting to the executive steering committee. This same team (or a new team) would then be responsible for introducing the BSC to the organization and installing the lower-level metrics within departments and their constituent work groups (on the primary visual display of each intact work group). If an organization larger than a single site wishes to implement a BSC, a corporate-level change team (with management representation from the sites) should develop the high-level BSC and then promulgate it to the sites. Each site would then have its BSC change team conduct the implementation.

VALUE STREAM MAPPING

General Description—Value stream mapping (VSM) is a highly structured and standardized flowcharting methodology that focuses on cycle times and waiting (lead) times as well as queues. As might be expected, there is no one "right" way to do value stream mapping. Nor is there any one organization or process level at which it is applied. Value stream mapping has been applied to an entire organization, a customer call center, or a sales order process.

Strengths—If done properly, VSM discovers and builds consensus about both the structure of a process (of whatever scope) and areas that, if given attention, will create substantial value by speeding up processes and eliminating non-valued-added work. It is an excellent analysis tool.

Best Integration Approach—As with the BSC, VSM is only a tool. Its popularity has led many managers and executives to assume that the mere use of VSM will lead to a transformation of all processes and leadership approaches. It can be tremendously effective in providing focus but it cannot be expected to magically change the individual leadership styles and daily behaviors of supervisors and managers. Therefore, it must be paired with an approach that provides structure, discipline, and ownership: Office Kaizen. The prior or simultaneous introduction of an organizationwide balanced scorecard would do a lot to align managers with the mission of VSM. All VSM exercises should be conducted by chartered teams that report either to the executive steering committee of a site or a department steering committee (if the department is large) or by a kaizen blitz team (administered by a team reporting to the executive steering committee). There's no sense in wasting time if there is not a clear purpose and management oversight to assure follow-up.

REENGINEERING/CONTINUOUS IMPROVEMENT

General Description—Reengineering, lionized by many books, is a body of tools that is applied to analyze and fix processes. These tools can include value stream mapping, cross-functional teams, statistical methods, executive committees, and just about every recognizable business tool or approach. The more generic label of *continuous improvement* operates in the same manner. A continuous improvement effort often includes a group of managers or executives that identifies reengineering targets, establishes priorities, selects teams, and makes trade-off decisions. In poorly run efforts, teams sprout up randomly and reengineer whatever comes to mind. When they are planned, a selected team conducts the analysis and implements the changes. A "reengineering initiative" can encompass anything from an organizationwide overhaul to an individual department's attempts to fix a single process.

Strengths—Properly conducted, reengineering is a powerful body of tools that can produce tremendous improvements.

Best Integration Approach—When reengineering and continuous improvement are implemented in the correct manner, they employ many Office Kaizen methods (ESC, champions, chartered change teams, work group metrics, and so on). If a comprehensive reengineering and/or continuous improvement effort is being contemplated, leadership must make sure that the mechanisms within the effort provide focus, structure, discipline, and ownership at all levels of the organization.

SIX SIGMA

General Description—Sigma is a lower-case Greek letter, shown as σ. It is used as a symbol for a standard deviation, a measure of variability. The formal definition for σ is "the average distance between a score in a distribution and the average, or the mean, of the distribution." As a set of numbers in a distribution spreads out farther from its mean, the σ for the distribution increases. As σ increases, it becomes more difficult to predict where the next score will fall. This is akin to a golfer who shoots 75 some days and 110 on others; it is hard to say how they will fare next time. A golfer with a smaller σ is one that is more consistent around their average.

The expression "six sigma," or "6σ," represents a distance of six standard deviations between the average of a distribution and the closest specification limit. It is desirable to have a large safety margin in any process. This safety margin is expressed in terms of σ multiples. Six sigma is the gold standard for such a process outcome, because the odds are millions to one that a stable process with a 6σ distance between the mean and the closest specification limit will produce a single bad output. A six sigma process is synonymous with a process capability (or C_{pk}) of 2.0.

Six Sigma, as a program, has a heavy dose of statistics in its DNA. The approach was born at Motorola in the 1980s as a result of several forces. At the time, there was a lot of attention being devoted to benchmarking, measurement at the process level, concerns for quality, and the Japanese threat to the electronics industry. There was also a push for more statistical process controls as a result of Dr. Deming's proselytizing. There was concurrent fascination with design of experiments (see the later section on DOE and Shainin) as a tool. Finally, there was a lot of interest in structured problem-solving approaches that required the use of cause-and-effect diagrams, problem definitions, and Pareto charts. Many of these tools came together in an approach that Motorola named "Six Sigma," in that the goal was to attain 6σ levels for all critical processes. Six Sigma migrated out of Motorola and is offered by several "licensed" organizations and countless corporations who have developed their own versions.

Essentially, Six Sigma is a program that brings together a number of problem-solving statistical methods and reliability tools in a package that includes some guidelines for effective management of process improvement/problem-solving efforts. In order to provide pride and enthusiasm for the early practitioners, Six Sigma employed the concept of colored belts (analogous to those awarded to martial arts trainees) to denote levels of mastery. Master Blackbelts (the highest level) are senior executives who sponsor Six Sigma projects and/or provide advanced project management and design of experiments support. At the other end are Yellowbelts. These are employees who have mastered basic problem solving and statistical tools.

Strengths—The statistical tools of Six Sigma are obviously very powerful. It is a great approach for processes in which slight variability can greatly impact outcomes. These include industrial processes like machining, tooling (where tolerances and "tolerance stack-up" are critical), and chemical processing. When applied to less "statistical" problems, Six Sigma is only as good as the problem-solving approaches employed and the general knowledge and skills of the practitioners, which vary infinitely between individuals, Six Sigma programs, and company constraints.

Best Integration Approach—Six Sigma can be a nuclear blowtorch of process improvement heat when directed at problems that require burning. Yet, a blowtorch is not the tool of choice if the task is pitching hay. Six Sigma practitioners, if let loose upon an organization without focus and structure, often attempt to use their blowtorches for every task. It is imperative that the efforts of Six Sigma experts (and all other tool practitioners) be carefully directed and monitored by an informed executive steering committee. The key for management is to provide focus, structure, and discipline in the use of all tools and methods, however well known or famous they may be. This means that Six Sigma tools should be applied only with the benefit of a chartered change team that reports to an executive steering committee.

LEAN MANUFACTURING

General Description—Lean manufacturing is the generic term given to applications of the Toyota Production System (TPS). The TPS is variously labeled as lean, flexible, pull, cellular, synchronous, one-by-one, or demand–flow manufacturing. Constraint management is a variation of lean manufacturing applied to specific instances (despite what its often fanatical adherents contend). The bottom-line objective of a lean system is to dramatically reduce the seven wastes first outlined by Taiichi Ohno. The wastes are processing (doing something in a non-optimum manner), motion, waiting, inventory, making too much (or work-in-process), moving things, and fixing defects. The entire system of workplace organization, fast die changes, pull signals, lot size reductions, and so on, is designed to continually reduce instances of waste. The emphasis is to reduce waste through the efforts of hands-on workers in small groups (often called cells).

Strengths—The very considerable power of this approach is based on three factors: 1) it is a proven structure that supplies worksheets and methodologies that get results fast (the method assumes waste and attacks it without studying it, which is almost always very, very effective); 2) it operates well at the level of the hands-on workers where most of the small instances of waste occur (and are not visible to most managers); and 3) it quickly produces results on the bottom line. Part of the power of lean manufacturing in plant areas is that its methods package a great deal of focus, structure, and discipline within many of its tools. Applied properly, it also creates considerable ownership among hands-on workers.

Best Integration Appraoch—Lean manufacturing is the single most effectively integrated body of tools that can be applied to a production or manufacturing process. However, it does not deal well with complex process control (reliability, variability) problems and it is not designed to solve complicated problems, especially those that operate across cell or department lines. Further, while its basic philosophy (elimination of waste, cells, pull rather than push) applies to all work, the standard tools of lean manufacturing are much less effective when taken out of the factory and applied to office processes without considerable modification. When lean manufacturing is being implemented, the same management structure of Office Kaizen's executive steering committee, champions, chartered change teams, and the LDMS must be employed for maximum results.

PROJECT MANAGEMENT

General Description—As organizations get larger, they automatically tend in the direction of less efficient communication, coordination, and consensus building. To put it another way, as they get larger, organizations generate more focus, structure, discipline, and ownership waste in their project management efforts (and everything else). It does not matter whether the project is ISO certification, reengineering, or value stream mapping. Formal project management methods attempt to overcome this difficulty by mandating processes and structure for significant change efforts. Some organizations are content to simply force every project member to use the same off-the-shelf project software. Others opt for even more complicated planning packages. Some approaches are heavy on team meetings and discussions; others focus heavily on twice or thrice weekly management review sessions.

Strengths—In the land of the severely sight challenged, the slightly myopic (or presbyopic) are the rulers. If an organization has run projects with cursory management attention, and/or loosely structured/supported project teams, and/or irregular project reviews, almost anything, including complicated software, may help. Almost anything is not acceptable for high-performance, much less world-class project management. Good project management approaches demand chartered teams, management oversight and review, and appropriate tools. In short, good project management is Office Kaizen's change team approach (and vice-versa).

Best Integration Approach—Project management approaches typically do little to change the structure of everyday work where the project must be sustained. It is critical that the project change team (cross-functional, chartered, and championed, of course) be tasked to install the appropriate measures, training, and procedures in each intact work group that is affected by the project. Every primary visual display within impacted intact work groups must have measures on it that the work group can use to monitor how well it is maintaining the installed processes. The smart leader eschews project management approaches that rely heavily on software. Software-driven efforts are always victimized by "cubicle commissars." These apparatchiks are enthusiasts who enjoy spending all of their time manipulating schedules and generating beautiful PowerPoint presentations on "project status" rather than doing hands-on work with project teams and intact work groups.

ISO 9000/QS-9000

General Description—ISO 9000 is a product of the International Organization for Standardization that evolved during the 1980s. QS-9000 is an adaptation and slight elaboration of ISO 9000 that was developed by Ford, Chrysler, and General Motors in the late 1980s and early 1990s. Small modifications and changes in both are continuous. Each consists of a set of minimum standards for the operation of key processes, such as: management's role in managing quality, contract review, design control, inspection and test status, and training. QS more or less mirrors ISO but also has sections that are automotive industry–specific, as well as sections specific to Ford, Chrysler, and General Motors. The automakers compelled their suppliers to become certified "or else." The certification is performed by sending auditors (who work, usually as independent contractors, for a small number of official "registrar" companies) to visit the candidate organization and review documentation and processes. Organizations who pass are certified. Those who fail must try again. The "9000" label refers to the general standard (what it is). Those who are certified "9001" are organizations who design, manufacture, and service a product. Those who manufacture and service the product (no design) are certified "9002" and those who provide only a service (such as a consulting company) would be certified "9003." Various other "numbers" apply to more esoteric portions of the standard. Organizations that are certified must be recertified on a regular basis (every year or two).

Strengths—The most powerful aspect of the "9000" programs is the emphasis on minimum acceptable practices as a standard. Once an organization's "ticket is punched," it has passed a major supplier selection hurdle. The intent of these "9000" programs is to provide a minimum level of functioning for key processes. The "9000" programs can make a big difference in organizations where such attention was either sparse or altogether lacking prior to the certification effort. To the extent that an industry (such as the U.S. automotive industry) uses certification as a selection criterion for suppliers, the standard provides a common framework for expectations and process structure. At the same time, almost every organization that is in serious trouble due to unimaginable waste and poor performance is either ISO or QS certified (as are those that are not in trouble; certification does not predict high performance because "everybody" is certified).

Best Integration Approach—In order to "do certification right," an organization (site) should charter teams to develop the various elements (or sets of elements) of the standard. This assures executive review and coaching on a weekly basis. Each team must be responsible for driving its efforts down to the intact work group level (this is the major shortfall of most ISO/QS implementations; the documentation looks great but most of the employees haven't seen it and don't abide by it).

DOE/SHAININ

General Description—Experimental design techniques were developed in the 1920s by the English statistician Robert Fisher and others. They developed somewhat complex methods (to non-statisticians) to ascertain the impact of several variables (things that can be manipulated) on a desired outcome. Design of experiments (DOE) is the name most commonly applied to Genichi Taguchi's approach for simplifying these techniques for engineers. Taguchi took certain types of designs that were very efficient and reduced them to "cookbook" methods that can be applied (to some extent) by engineers after a week or two of training. Dorian Shainin also developed a "cookbook" approach that requires users to do quite a bit more up-front cause-and-effect exploration as an integral part of the methodology. While anyone can learn and apply general experimental design methods in any manner that suits them, Shainin methods are tightly packaged and controlled by the company founded by the late Dorian Shainin. Extensive training and certification takes an acolyte through several levels of training (including continuing education).

Strengths—These techniques are extremely powerful and parsimonious with resources. If the right questions are asked in the correct manner, these techniques can produce tremendous improvements in processes with minimum expenditures on new technology and/or equipment.

Best Integration Approach—It is hard to imagine a situation in an office environment where these techniques would apply (that would make sense; I could invent a situation that would demonstrate the technique but it would be pointless in the real world). If such an application is proposed, it is imperative that the executive steering committee carefully determines that such a tool applies.

INTEGRATED PRODUCT DEVELOPMENT (IPD)

General Description—IPD might be loosely described as reengineering for design engineering and product development personnel and processes. As with reengineering, IPD means something different for everyone who practices it. The tools and the methods of IPD are drawn from many sources, almost all of them with a technical and/or engineering ancestry. The grandfather of these technical approaches is called quality function deployment (QFD). QFD requires hundreds of meetings to develop what are called the "four houses of quality" in order to move from subjective customer requirements to the design of manufacturing processes. Each house is a massive cross-index of requirements, assessments, and attributes. I have never seen an organization apply more than 15 percent of the model; there is simply too much structure imposed on too many people without ownership. Many IPD approaches are based upon Boothroyd and Dewhurst's proprietary design for assembly (DFA) methodology that assesses design characteristics vis-à-vis ease of assembly (automated and/or manual). This approach provides focus and structure for a design team and leads to assemblies with fewer parts and faster, more efficient manufacturing processes.

Strengths—The IPD methodologies described above (and many others) are outstanding at providing individuals and teams with a focus on a number of key design criteria that might not otherwise be exhaustively analyzed. In effect, they provide a balanced scorecard for design.

Best Integration Approach—The missing elements in most IPD approaches involve management involvement, focus, and structure, and the creation of ownership among the design personnel. A design initiative must be structured as a mini–executive steering committee/change team effort. Each design team (or the sole design team) must have a specific charter that is agreed-upon by a cross-functional management team. In a small site or organization, the executive steering committee is this management team and there might be only one design team. In a large organization with many design initiatives, the executive steering committee for a specific design team may in fact be a cross-functional management team assembled to oversee and direct the specific design effort. In this case, each of several change teams reporting to the management team would be responsible for a specific element of the design. Needless to say (but I will anyway), each individual design team must be chartered and championed *and* have its own lean daily management system (including the KCG 20 Keys of IPD).

ENTERPRISE SOFTWARE

General Description—It is not surprising, given our dependence on and fascination with computers, that technology-based solutions get a lot of serious attention as possible weapons against any and all business problems. Everybody would like to find the magic bullet that would solve many problems with one keystroke or mouse click. Enterprise software, often called enterprise information software (EIS), is the fullest expression of this hunger. Three of the many well-known vendors of EIS systems are SAP, BAAN, and PeopleSoft. These software companies sell comprehensive sets of software modules for various elements of a business. There are modules for manufacturing, customer service, financials, engineering, purchasing, and human resources, to name a few. The modules "talk" to one another. The intent is to provide a single system that integrates all the knowledge, status, and information in an organization so that management (and others) can quickly determine what, where, and when things are happening without a lot of trouble. In theory, a perfect EIS would provide an incredibly detailed balanced scorecard for all levels of an organization that would be based upon real time (or close to it) data from all other parts of the organization. Unfortunately, few (if any) installations realize this goal. Many organizations purchase the systems because they are popular, they want to "keep up with the Joneses," or EIS is touted as "the answer."

Strengths—EIS can be very helpful if the information is critical, is acted upon wisely, and provides more value than it costs to collect.

Best Integration Approach—All software implementations must be conducted by chartered change teams reporting to an executive steering committee. It is critical that the teams be cross-functional so that the decisions are not the sole providence of the IT department. Nevertheless, even cross-functional teams may not prevent the most disastrous problem: a failure to appreciate how expensive and time consuming it is to write custom software. Many organizations believe that their processes are unique. Instead of changing processes, they compel the installers to write software to enable the "canned" EIS modules to communicate with their "legacy" systems. This gets very expensive very fast. The expense grows every time an old in-house system must be replaced or the new version of the software is installed. Leadership (the executive steering committee) is responsible for mandating charters that minimize customization for all but life or death process issues. An additional integration issue is use of the system after it is installed. Software programs, unless implanted in the brain, cannot compel behavior. Intact work groups that use and maintain the software must track their software use performance on a regular basis. Only this and continual training and coaching will maintain the integrity of the software performance.

FINAL COMMENTS

The underlying message of this chapter is that "tools are tools" and that leadership is the foundation that permits all tools to operate to their full potential. Leadership must require that all tool applications be applied with the necessary focus, structure, discipline, and ownership at each organization level. The executive steering committee (with champions, charters, and change teams) and the lean daily management system are the most parsimonious approach to providing this framework.

11

The Lens for Focus: Metrics

George's team continued to review the elements of Office Kaizen and their implementation concerns. They were pleased with the book's candid discussion of the "usual tools" and appreciated that although every approach was afforded value, none were described as "perfect." They had all been repeatedly burned by "magic bullet" quests in the past. At the same time, the group was concerned about making sure that important business processes would be attended to while Office Kaizen was being installed. "After all," George observed, "we still have a business to run and profits to generate. Our shareholders aren't going to cut us any slack just because we're trying to 'get better' in the future. We'll have to make certain that we keep everybody focused on their key processes and performance targets even as we implement Office Kaizen." They began to read the chapter on metrics.

The fourth compression band of the SLIM-IT conceptual model (Figure 6.1, page 65) is *metrics*. The term has become popular, most likely because it sounds more technical than "measurement." Over the past decade or so, "metric" has evolved to the point where it is generally thought to be a more precise, meaningful, and accurate characterization of a process or situation than that provided by a lowly "measurement." In fact, most of what are called either metrics or measurements are generally poor or pedestrian at best. Some are dangerous. Since many businesspeople expect and/or suppose that metrics are "better" than measurements, Office Kaizen takes advantage of this existing expectation and defines metrics quite specifically:

> A metric is a measure that provides vital information about important issues, the status of ongoing efforts, and progress (or lack of it) to a person or group who can significantly impact the measure through direct, hands-on, micro-process efforts.

The key word here is "impact." If the person or group that is presented with the measurement cannot do something significant to affect it, it is not a metric for the group or person. For them, and for others who collect or monitor, such a measure is only information, and often not good information—a measurement. Why look at something if you cannot do anything about it? Each of the measures shown in Table 11.1 is a metric because the person or group presented with it can have a direct impact on it within a reasonable time. The elements shown in Table 11.2 are only measurements, because the person or group presented with the information has little hope of making a significant impact on the measurement solely through their efforts over the short to medium term.

Table 11.1 Measures that are metrics.

Metric	Person or Group
Number of purchase orders processed each day	Individual buyer
Cycle time to complete a software revision	The programming intact work group given the assignment and the change team tasked to reduce the cycle time
Percent reduction in new hire cycle time	The change team tasked to reengineer the hiring value stream and the intact work group that adopts the new process
Number of customer inquiry calls returned the same day by a section	The intact work group making the calls
Accuracy of a sales order	The salesperson completing the order
Number of order entry errors by group	The intact work group of order entry personnel
Labor costs per unit of sales	Any intact work group

Table 11.2   Measures that are not metrics.

Measurement	Person or Group
Stock price of the corporation	Any department or person (or even an entire site in a large organization)
Overhead site costs or site labor costs	Any individual worker or department
Percent of employees voting to join a union	Any individual manager
Customer satisfaction with the overall service or product from a site	Any individual worker or department
Cost of quality lost	The quality department or any individual department or worker
Employee morale for a site (by survey)	Any individual manager

THE PLACE OF METRICS IN SLIM-IT

The central portion of Figure 6.2 illustrates "running the business." Note the two-way arrows that connect the central portion of the figure with the LDMS. The LDMS provides the means for measures to become metrics. That is, metrics must operate at the level at which action can be taken. For most of the people in an organization, this means that metrics must operate at the intact work group level via the LDMS. For example, let's assume that one site of a multi-site organization is experiencing a good deal of labor strife. As a result, a union organizing effort is underway at the unfortunate site. The corporate office of the organization tracks periodic employee survey information as to how many employees are pro-union in various sites. Is that measurement a metric for the manager of the site with labor troubles? Is such a measure a metric for a supervisor at the site?

In a traditional environment, the answer to both questions is no; the site manager would have little leverage to reduce the pro-union percentage in a short to medium (one to three months) time period. Without the LDMS, a supervisor or lead would have equally little leverage. You could make the argument that the percentage of pro-union votes would function as a long-term metric for the site manager in an Office Kaizen environment; a stable or increasing pro-union percentage would be a reflection of the site manager's lack of progress in implementing and/or maintaining Office Kaizen over a period of two to three years. This is because Office Kaizen is a union avoidance strategy; it provides workers with more of what they really want out of work (respect, power, pride, and so on) whether they consciously realize it or not.

In an Office Kaizen environment, changes in the percentage of pro-union votes within an individual work group would be a metric as to how good a job the supervisor or lead was doing in implementing the LDMS. However, in either case, the percentage of votes is a marginally effective metric because it is too "far" away from the action. It would be far better to measure the site manager (and any individual supervisor) as to how well they were implementing the elements of the LDMS. Thus, a predictive union avoidance metric for a site manager would be "the percentage of work groups that are holding daily work group meetings" and "the percentage of work groups that have a KCG 20 Keys assessment and plan in place." If these numbers are high, the pro-union votes will decrease.

This is the magic of SLIM-IT; it provides the means (structure and discipline) for management to be accountable and to pass the appropriate responsibility for metrics down to the work group level where they can be influenced (focus and ownership). In an Office Kaizen environment, the employees are too involved in their work to be seduced by the "magic answer" that union membership often suggests. An organization employing Office Kaizen already provides employees with most of what they really want: involvement, commitment, a sense of worth and achievement, inclusion in decision making and direct communication, and involvement with leadership (on change and blitz teams).

While the end goal of Office Kaizen is to produce an environment in which surface waste is dramatically reduced and continuously reduced over the long term, this can only be achieved through the relentless reduction of the leadership wastes of focus, structure, discipline, and ownership at every level of the organization. Without a mechanism such as SLIM-IT in place, an organization will not get consistent and enduring leadership waste reduction. Surface waste will endure. Metrics are great, but they have to be delivered correctly; the best injectable antibiotic in the world does little when it is applied as a hair conditioner.

WHAT MAKES A GOOD METRIC?

A metric does not exist in isolation. A metric assesses one dimension of the performance of an individual, a process, a work group, or a location. That is, each metric reflects a portion of the overall performance of a complicated situation. No one metric can tell the whole story and no metric can be determined to be effective without considering the totality of inputs, outputs, causes, and effects of the situation in which it is used. A good metric can variously assess, predict, measure, or analyze a portion of an outcome. This means that a specific metric might do some things well and others not so well. The more "good" things a metric does, the better it is. The "goodness" of a metric can be determined by assessing it on a number of straightforward characteristics. These characteristics are:

Actionality—Actionality increases as the inputs that impact the metric come under the direct hands-on control of the people who are responsible for the performance of the metric.

Proximality—Proximality increases as a metric moves closer (in physical proximity and time) to the performance of the process, site, or work group that it assesses.

Immediacy—Immediacy increases as the time between changes in the inputs to the performance and the metric decrease.

Causality—Causality increases as a metric assesses a cause rather than an effect of the overall performance of the individual, site, process, or work group being targeted. For example, total sales dollars achieved for an inside sales group is more of an effect than a cause of long-term, high-quality performance by the group. The number of proactive phone calls made by the group to existing customers is more of a cause of long-term, high-quality performance than an effect of it. Both are good metrics but causes are always better.

Proportionality—Proportionality increases as changes in the performance of the individual, work group, site, or process have a direct statistical relationship (a high correlation, positive or negative) with the metric. That is, if something is done to move the inputs to the desired process in a positive direction, the metric changes accurately reflect the relative strength of those efforts.

Atechnology—Atechnology increases as the ease with which a metric can be updated and understood by the people responsible for improving it increases.

Teamness—Teamness increases as a metric engages intact work groups (or change teams) in meaningful, focused improvement efforts more than it engages individuals.

Customer Focus—Customer focus increases as a metric reflects performance relative to internal and/or external customer requirements rather than "business" concerns (such as profits) or bureaucratic reporting concerns (such as number of suggestions submitted across the corporation in a given year). This is not to say that "profits" are not important, but rather that profits arise from doing the cost-effective things that customers require.

Let's examine several common measurements and see how they stack up against these eight metric characteristics. We'll assume that we are dealing with measurements at one site of a multi-site, publicly traded corporation. We will use a three-point scale to assess each of the eight characteristics:

2 = meets the characteristic extremely well or a lot

1 = meets the characteristic a little

0 = does not meet the characteristic

Table 11.3 presents an assessment of six metrics. The first three (from left to right) are measurements often thought important (in that they are tracked and prominently displayed in many traditionally run organizations). Metrics four through six are common to Office Kaizen environments. The measures are defined as follows:

Stock price	Daily closing stock price for the corporation
Site errors per day	Total daily processing errors for all work groups at the site
Site sales per month	Total sales dollars for the site each month
Daily order accuracy	Percent correct line items from a single intact work group in internal sales
KCG 20 Keys score	Current score for a single intact work group in internal sales
Order throughput time	Average order processing time of a sample of randomly selected orders each day from a single intact work group of internal sales personnel

The assessment of the goodness of each metric is conducted from the perspective of two different work groups:

a. Any one or all of the site management team (EX)

b. An intact work group within inside sales/service at the site (IWG)

As Table 11.3 clearly shows, none of the traditional measures (one to three) make very good metrics. They are simply too little, too late, and too far from the action for either executives or the members of an intact work

Table 11.3 Assessment of six "metrics" from the perspective of different employees

Metric Characteristic	Representative Metrics/Measurements											
	1 Stock Price		2 Site Errors/ Day		3 Site Sales/ Month		4 Daily Order Accuracy		5 KCG 20 Keys Score		6 Order Through-put Time	
a = EX; b = IWG	a	b	a	b	a	b	a	b	a	b	a	b
Actionality	0	0	0	1	0	1	0	2	0	2	0	2
Proximality	0	0	0	1	0	1	0	2	0	2	0	2
Immediacy	0	0	0	0	0	0	0	2	0	1	0	2
Causality	0	0	0	0	0	0	0	0	0	2	0	0
Independence	0	0	0	0	0	0	0	1	0	1	0	1
Atechnology	0	0	0	0	0	0	1	2	2	2	1	2
Teamness	0	0	1	0	1	0	0	2	0	2	0	2
Customer focus	0	0	1	1	0	0	2	2	1	1	2	2
Total Points	**0**	**0**	**2**	**3**	**1**	**2**	**3**	**13**	**3**	**13**	**3**	**13**

group. The three Office Kaizen metrics (four to six) are excellent metrics for the intact work group but poor management metrics. This is key: it makes no sense for management to track things over which it has no direct control.

For example, what would a traditional management team do if it found that order throughput time (metric six in Table 11.3) was poor in an intact work group (that was not measuring the performance themselves)? They would most likely mandate action of some sort without in-depth knowledge of the area or the process. If management cannot take direct action itself, why are they measuring it? The correct approach is to implement metrics within the work area that allow appropriate action to be taken by the intact work group *without management being aware of the problem*. Good management metrics in this situation would assess how well management implements, coaches, and maintains such a system.

LEADERSHIP AND MANAGEMENT METRICS

The discussion of metrics almost always brings up an additional important facet of performance: how best to assess leadership and management performance? This is vitally important because Office Kaizen environments cannot be implemented or sustained without real leaders. Real leadership performance is rarely included in most organizations' evaluations of managers and supervisors. Most organizations' evaluations don't even hold managers responsible for the performance of their areas; it is rare to find a very low-rated manager even in organizations that are performing abysmally and have been on the decline for several years. If such circumstances do not indicate poor leadership, nothing does. Because most measures of leadership/management activity are poor metrics, it is possible for a manager to be rated as an outstanding performer in many cases simply by attaining a number of completely irrelevant objectives. It was this realization that drove much of the energy behind the balanced scorecard approach.

Office Kaizen provides an answer to this disconnect between what is measured and what should be measured. The true measure of a manager is how well they provide focus, structure, discipline, and ownership at all levels of the organization (to the extent that he or she has control); that is, how well they sustain Office Kaizen. Table 11.4 assesses six such metrics using the eight metric characteristics that were introduced with Table 11.3. The performance that is being assessed by the metrics is "the creation/maintenance of a maximally effective workforce" at the site. The metrics shown in the table are:

Attend ESC meetings = Attendance and participation at executive steering committee meetings.

"Patrol" PVD & DWGM = Monitoring and observing the operation and status of primary visual displays and daily work group meetings. Coaching of management and supervisors as required.

Champion/coach change teams = Acting as champion to one or more change teams and coaching them in charter development, status presentations, and change implementation.

KCG 20 Keys Site score = Total average site score (average of all intact work groups per key and/or lowest common denominator of all intact work groups per key).

Maintain & coach PVD and DWGM = Coaching of the primary visual display and daily work group operation and improvement.

Maintain & coach KAS system = Coaching of the kaizen action sheet system within each intact work group.

Table 11.4 Assessment of Office Kaizen leadership metrics.

Metric Characteristic	Representative Office Kaizen Leadership Metrics																	
	1 Attend ESC Meetings			2 "Patrol" PVD & DWGM			3 Champion/ Coach Change Teams			4 KCG 20 Keys Site Score			5 Maintain & Coach PVD & DWGM			6 Maintain & Coach KAS System		
See legend below*	a	b	c	a	b	c	a	b	c	a	b	c	a	b	c	a	b	c
Actionality	2	n	n	1	2	n	2	n	n	0	1	2	1	1	2	0	1	2
Proximality	1	n	n	1	2	n	2	n	n	0	1	1	1	1	2	0	1	2
Immediacy	1	n	n	1	2	n	1	n	n	0	1	1	1	1	2	0	1	1
Causality	2	n	n	1	1	n	2	n	n	1	1	1	1	1	2	1	1	1
Independence	2	n	n	1	1	n	1	n	n	0	0	1	2	2	2	0	0	2
Atechnology	2	n	n	2	2	n	2	n	n	2	2	2	2	2	2	2	2	2
Teamness	2	n	n	1	1	n	2	n	n	2	2	2	1	1	1	2	2	2
Customer focus	1	n	n	1	1	n	1	n	n	1	1	1	1	1	1	0	1	1
Total Points	13	n	n	9	12	n	13	n	n	6	9	14	6	10	15	5	9	13

*a = site manager or direct reports to the site manager

b = a middle manager with a few direct reports

c = a supervisor/lead of an intact work group

DWGM = daily work group meeting

KAS = kaizen action sheet system (improvement suggestion program run within an intact work group)

n = does not apply

PVD = primary visual display

The assessment of each metric is done from the perspective of three different types of personnel:

a. The site manager or direct reports to the site manager

b. A middle manager with a few direct reports

c. A supervisor/lead of an intact work group

We will apply the same three-point scale as used for Table 11.3 to assess each of the eight characteristics:

2 = meets the characteristic extremely well or a lot

1 = meets the characteristic a little

0 = does not meet the characteristic

Note that the executive scores for metrics four through six are lower than those for metrics one to three. This is as expected. Metrics four through six assess intact work group function. While executives can do some coaching, it is not as "close" (proximity, immediacy, and independence) to the work group as the same activities conducted by supervisors or leads. The supervisor's/lead's good metric is only a fair to poor metric (but still good enough to be a metric rather than a measurement) for an executive.

Metrics one to three demonstrate the absolute criticality of the leadership function. Note that these three metrics are direct assessments of how well the executives are nurturing the overall structure of SLIM-IT (the outer band of Figure 6.1). While middle managers can provide some assistance in patrolling primary visual displays and daily work group meetings, the installation and structure of Office Kaizen at a site depends upon executive leadership. Of course, if executives abrogate this function, metrics four through six would be pointless; there would be no structure for the supervisors and leads to maintain and improve upon.

COSTS ARE NOT GOOD METRICS

Most traditional managers and organizations attempt to manage waste indirectly by managing costs. They assume that if costs are continually reduced and the business continues to function, the process must be squeezing out inefficiencies. If this were the case, almost every organization would, by now, be operating at world-class levels. What organization has not undergone a cost-cutting scheme and then continued (and continues today) to fall victim to the same old problems? These problems occur because the bulk of surface waste is directly bound to its processes; cost cutting eliminates good, necessary work as well as waste.

Costs have always been popular as measurements because they are easy to measure (although they are not easy to measure at the level that would be useful) and are "management owned"; that is, management can operate under the illusion that by managing costs, they are running the business. This is a foolish and dangerous illusion. Managing costs is too little, too late, too distant, too confounded, and too general to be anything but eyewash. Almost all cost measures, if assessed against the eight metrics characteristics presented earlier, would fare abysmally. Instead of costs, management must demand that metrics be generated from cause-and-effect diagrams that identify *the causes of costs at the hands-on work level.*

INTERNAL AND EXTERNAL CUSTOMERS

While most managers may not be focused on surface waste (or even be aware of it as a strategic issue), they do know that customers want better "everything" even if the only customer they are thinking about is their boss. Unfortunately, as we have seen, traditional managers have little leverage to obtain such results with the measurements they have been using. They are like 19th century engineers struggling to achieve powered flight; they know what they want, have seen it done (birds, bats, insects), but don't have the technology to do it themselves. Without Office Kaizen, modern managers face the same lack of technology in attempting to satisfy their most important customers.

As mentioned in chapter 3, a perfectly wise, all-knowing customer would not tolerate paying for waste if they had a choice. This customer desires the best product or service for their purpose at the best price (determined by lifecycle or one-time usage, frequency of purchase, and so on). Fortunately for most businesses, there are no such customers to jam up the service center phones. All customers pay for a great deal of waste whether they like it or not and whether they know about it or not. If they were able to locate a supplier with lower costs, better service, and the same or better quality, their business would migrate over time to the new supplier (marketing fogs the process and slows down the migration).

Everything should be driven by customer requirements whether the customers are internal or external to the organization. External customer requirements receive a lot of lip service and, in the last few years, an increasing amount of meaningful attention in many organizations. Yet, the big savings are hidden elsewhere. The overwhelming amount of office and administrative work performed in most organizations never directly touches a customer. Most office tasks support internal customers, who in turn support other internal customers. Eventually, the value chain reaches an external customer, but comparatively few office and administrative workers touch one directly. If the external customers do not complain, massive amounts of waste can remain among the internal customers' processes.

Internal customers do not even receive lip service in traditional environments. If internal customers could read the minds of their internal suppliers they would see, in most organizations, at best, disinterest, and, at worst, contempt. Yet, this is where the bulk of surface waste is created and passed along to customers. Every tiny internal customer requirement that is short-changed is magnified as it is passed from person to area to work group. The end result is a missed service introduction, a bad design, a late software upgrade, a missed delivery commitment, higher prices, and quality problems. There is a vast reservoir of waste hidden beneath the parched desert of internal customer dissatisfaction. The secret divining rod to locating and quantifying this ocean of wasted profit is metrics at the proper level. With the right metrics, SLIM-IT can pump the reservoir of waste to the surface and use it to transform the desert of dissatisfaction into a blooming garden of customer satisfaction and profit.

What do internal customers want? The same five needs that everybody at work (and in life in general) wants—need satisfaction in the form of survival, belongingness, power, fun, and freedom. A number of these needs can be satisfied by metrics working via SLIM-IT. Some are dependent on management determination and leadership, and some of them have multiple contributors. A few of them, and the means by which they are addressed in an Office Kaizen environment, are displayed in Table 11.5.

Management must help each intact work group put in place metrics that focus on enabling it to:

1. Make it easy for its upstream suppliers to give it what it needs

2. Provide downstream customers with what they need

If these are done in a SLIM-IT environment, surface wastes will begin to decline immediately and will continue to decline. While SLIM-IT provides many clues to generic metrics via the KCG 20 Keys, each work group's supervision must help it establish on-target metrics as a starting point. After a couple of months, the work groups will take over and develop more and improved metrics.

Table 11.5   Internal customer requirements, needs, and methods of satisfaction.

Requirement	In-Born Need(s) Satisfied	How Satisfied
Clear direction as to what is required	Survival, Belonging	ESC Meetings, LDMS, Leadership, KCG 20 Keys
Understanding of how success is measured	Survival, Belonging	Charters, KCG 20 Keys, Metrics
Clear and strong leadership	Survival, Power, Freedom	ESC, ESC Champions, Mentors
Ability to distinguish the irrelevant from the critical	Power, Freedom	LDMS, Metrics, KCG 20 Keys
Some control of their fate	Freedom	ESC Champions, LDMS, Change Teams, KCG 20 Keys
Power to make reasonable decisions that affect them	Power	LDMS, Change Teams, KCG 20 Keys
Understanding of how their efforts fit into the big picture	Survival, Power, Freedom	ESC, ESC Champions, LDMS, Mentors, Change Teams, KCG 20 Keys
Knowledge to do what is required	Survival, Power, Freedom	ESC Champions, Mentors, LDMS, Metrics
Materials and the means to do what is required	Survival, Power, Freedom	ESC, ESC Champions, LDMS, Mentors, Change Teams, Training, Metrics
Recognition for achieving goals	Fun, Power	ESC, ESC Champions, LDMS, Mentors, Metrics, KCG 20 Keys
Value as creative, intelligent human beings	Belonging, Power, Freedom, Fun	ESC, ESC Champions, LDMS, Mentors, KCG 20 Keys

FINAL COMMENTS

There is no rocket science to good metrics; just hard work that demands and sustains a structure that reaches down into every intact work group. Without such a structure and management support, no measurement can function as a metric. Metrics function because they provide a means of leading, not because they measure outputs.

12

The Realities
of Implementation

In their excitement at selecting work streams at the first ESC meeting for the corporate office site, the group didn't notice as George slipped out of the room. "I'm confident that my team can run the Office Kaizen effort here at headquarters," thought George, "and I'm confident we can give the right marching orders to the various offices and service centers around the country. But how do we support them? Where do we draw the line between micro-managing them and making sure that they are doing Office Kaizen the right way?"

K nowing what needs to be done is not the same as knowing how to do it. This chapter will discuss critical Office Kaizen implementation issues, pitfalls, and tactics. The suggestions and warnings in this chapter are, in principle, applicable to all initiatives and programs.

EACH SITE STANDS ALONE

A large organization with multiple locations is analogous to a fleet of warships; each ship is a separate entity that must battle and survive on its own. The fleet is run by an admiral who directs the overall fleet, but the admiral cannot assure the success of every ship every minute. That task must be left to the captains and crews of the individual ships. The fleet offers some advantage to every ship in the form of intimidation through numbers, sharing of knowledge, and perhaps special services that some ships do not possess. In the final analysis, each ship must live or die largely by its own initiative.

Organizations are the same. CEOs would be overjoyed to bring every business unit back to port unscathed at the conclusion of each successful fiscal year campaign. Yet, there are casualties every year. An occasional business unit sinks and many are damaged. The objective of a CEO is to bring back the most booty (profits) with the fewest losses. The CEO plans the campaign and the individual business units carry out the orders. The battles with the competition are fought product-to-product, service-to-service, and business unit–to–business unit.

Many organizations lose sight of this reality when they implement something new. They often attempt to simultaneously introduce and operate an initiative across the entire organization from atop the corporate mountain. While finding and mandating the use of necessary bold new ideas is one of the corporate office's most critical roles, the implementation must be owned and operated independently at each site. Corporate can mandate what must be done, but the sites must be responsible for *how* it is done.

The term *site* has been used many times in previous chapters. It is the largest single segment of an organization that can be overseen effectively by one executive steering committee (ESC). *Site* is typically analogous to a specific office building, office suite, campus, or center that contains one discrete unit of the organization. In organizations that have locations in many cities, the operation in each city is a site. However, if one campus contains 7000 people working for three distinct business segments with different teams of executives, there should be three separate Office Kaizen efforts at that one site. The ESC must be the "buck stops here" group for the implementation at a site. That is, the employees must view the people on the management team of the site (from which the ESC is drawn) as their organization's leaders.

THE ROLE OF LEADERSHIP AT VARIOUS LEVELS

The CEO or the top executive for the business segment and his staff have several critical duties:

1. Launch an Office Kaizen initiative at the corporate office site

2. Mandate that each site in the organization pursue Office Kaizen

3. Provide the site leaders with an introduction as to what Office Kaizen is and how it works

4. Give the site leaders an approximate timetable for completing required activities, such as:

   a. Form a functioning (weekly meetings) site executive steering committee by (date)

   b. Identify all change initiatives and establish formal teams, champions, leaders, and charters for the ones that are kept by (date)

   c. Implement the primary visual display and daily work group meeting (including the kaizen action sheet system) within 50 percent of intact work groups by (date)

   d. Complete primary visual display and daily work group meeting implementations by (date)

   e. Implement the KCG 20 Keys of Office Kaizen approach in all intact work groups by (date)

5. Require updates on implementation progress at normal site visits by executive staffers and at corporate during site executives' visits

6. Provide hands-on coaching resources to sites that need it (or insist that they obtain the resources on their own)

7. Quickly remove and replace site managers who cannot or will not get onboard

The site leader and other ESC members must (items for the site leader only are denoted by *):

1. Serve as the leader and mentor of the site ESC.*

2. Mentor the other members of the ESC and learn from them.

3. Quickly remove and replace staff members who cannot or will not get onboard.

4. Assure that team leaders and champions are doing their jobs.

5. Attend every ESC meeting unless otherwise unavoidable. If the site leader cannot be present, they must formally appoint one of the other members to lead the meeting.*

6. Make sure that all ESC members attend every meeting. If they have mandated travel, they must send a decision-making substitute.

7. Ensure that item four from the previous list (a. through e.) is implemented.

8. Attend at least one daily work group meeting every day and just observe.

9. Visit at least three primary visual displays every day and immediately talk to the intact work group leader if anything is not up to date.

10. Take every opportunity to recognize and applaud progress by any team or work group (such as completing a change or winning a point on the KCG 20 Keys).

11. Never stop pushing for slow, constant changes every day.

MISTAKES TO AVOID

1. *Not eliminating "concrete heads" quickly.* Almost without fail, executives who have led organizations to near or complete world-class status admit that their biggest mistake was "not getting rid of 'concrete heads' soon enough." These are the managers and executives that simply can't or won't get the message despite pleas and coaching. There aren't many of them, but they are poison. It is bad enough to try to change an organization with all the normal mistakes that well-intentioned people make. Allowing a "concrete head" to remain makes the journey 10 times more difficult. Just one or two of them can send enough bad signals to add 12 to 36 months to a site's climb to 60 points on the KCG 20 Keys. That's a lot of surface waste and lost profits. When a concrete head is encountered, be compassionate, caring, direct, and candid about what they must do. After three months, get rid of them.

2. *Measuring results of processes rather than measuring Office Kaizen implementation progress.* Do not create reporting requirements as to how many kaizen action sheets are submitted by each work group or how many points were picked up on the KCG 20 Keys last month. Instead, check out how many intact work groups have a primary visual display, are holding daily work group meetings, and have implemented the KCG 20 Keys of Office Kaizen. Do it in person at the sites (for a senior executive) and within departments (for the site manager).

3. *Using training to get started.* The typical in-house training function can do many things, but it cannot usually mentor managers day-to-day, especially in something like Office Kaizen, about which they know little. Training classes cannot be substituted for mentoring; the former is knowledge, the latter is coaching in real time.

4. *Not providing knowledgeable resources.* Some sites (and/or managers within a site) will need help. If they don't get it, they will flounder and damage the effort. Their failure will be viewed by others as the fault of the organization. The assistance must be provided in the form of mentoring as described in chapter 8, not simply encouragement or a training class. When asking people to change the basic structure of how they work and lead, a strategic competitive advantage cannot be had without expending resources.

5. *Giving the Office Kaizen initiative a name.* Once an initiative is given a name, it automatically assumes the stained, torn, and bloody mantle of all of the previous "programs" that briefly appeared and then died. No worthy effort of any kind should be forced to bear such a burden. Once it is given a name, most employees (and 99 percent of managers) will assume that the effort will be dead in six months. This will limit their involvement and enthusiasm. Simply announce that the organization is going to "try some new things." Just the savings from not purchasing coffee cups, plastic laminated wallet cards, hats, posters, and t-shirts should be enough to affect the bottom line right away.

6. *Allowing managers to "negotiate" fundamental changes in the structure of Office Kaizen.* Many strong leaders (site or department) think they know a lot about managing people and processes. Most know a lot about the traditional way. Do not allow strong personalities to forestall the implementation of a valid Office Kaizen initiative simply because they think they know a better way. There isn't one. A clever and energetic manager can get a lot of mileage out of strong leadership and the fire in their eyes. This is good, but it won't assure a long-term, strategic, competitive advantage. Leadership must do what is right to create a competitive advantage that outlives the individual leaders and their personal philosophies of management.

7. *Making a companywide announcement.* This has the same general effect as giving the initiative a name but is even more damaging. Announcements make everyone think (or hope or fear) that the initiative will get to them soon. If they are scared, they will be scared sooner and perhaps create more problems earlier. If they are hoping for improvement, they will be disappointed when the changes don't occur the next day. Let the sites or

departments allow events within them to explain themselves. Don't hide what's going on, but don't create a media frenzy that serves no purpose.

BRINGING IT ALL TOGETHER

Figure 12.1 presents the Office Kaizen Cube originally shown in Figure 2.3. Despite all of the material covered in this book, there's only one challenge: understanding and applying the Cube as a single, consistent approach to leadership.

Today's competitive market demands systematic, repeatable methods for achieving long-term, sustainable results and world-class performance. While technology and bold new innovations will continue to provide improvements and often be essential for success, everybody is squeezing those same lemons for the same juice. Office Kaizen provides an avenue that few will have the wisdom and will to apply.

If you know of another approach that can do what Office Kaizen promises, do it if it seems easier. You'll find that you are doing the same things that Office Kaizen advises but with less focus, structure, discipline, and ownership. Why try to reinvent parts of a wheel when the Office Kaizen formula-one, state-of-the-art, competitive racing machine awaits your driving skills? Don't forget to buckle up and don't forget to signal politely as you pass your competitors.

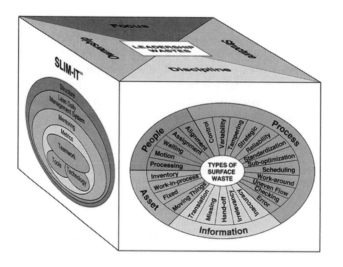

Figure 12.1   The Office Kaizen Cube.

Epilogue
Two Years Later . . .

It was 10 minutes until the board meeting. By some miracle of chaos, George was being left alone while others made decisions about last-minute details. Now that he thought about it, he realized that there was very little last-minute firefighting before meetings or events anymore. In fact, he hadn't had to handle a single, enraged "where is my shipment?" phone call from an angry CEO in the last month. Everything seemed to go smoother, yet so much faster. He knew why; he had just seen an example of it earlier this morning at the daily work group meeting he had attended in the corporate finance department.

The group had been reviewing its progress in resolving a problem it had faced in closing the European books for the month, which was the end of the quarter and the year. There was some issue about currency rates and a variety of bonds coming due; only finance people could understand it. The finance group had first heard about it three weeks earlier during one of their daily meetings. They had formed a "fix-it team" reporting to Corporate Office Location Executive Steering Committee. The team reported its progress to the ESC weekly and updated its progress each day on each of the finance areas' three primary visual display boards prior to each morning's work group meetings. With the fix-it team and everybody else aware of the issue and helping out, the problem had been resolved; the books for the year were closed on time and a new metric to track upcoming bond "something or others" had been added to the boards. It was almost like an automatic pilot was running things, even when there were problems.

George chuckled aloud at his use of the word "automatic." Two years ago, such a problem would have been a disaster. First of all, it wouldn't have been noticed before the end of the month. Then, just the blaming and finger-pointing would have taken two weeks. The books would have closed three to four weeks late, and it would have appeared to the market that the company was in trouble. It would have been, of course, but only because it was a typical organization, inundated with waste that few noticed until a problem surfaced.

These sorts of things didn't happen anymore, but getting there hadn't been easy. The last two years had been a whirlwind of change within a maelstrom of resistance amid a storm sea of chaos and mistakes. Yet, thinking back, from his current perspective as an Office Kaizen leader, he saw all the implementation problems as a normal part of the change process. At times he had been incensed by some of the resistance and posturing, but he had stayed the course. He, and most of his staff, had committed to maintaining the structural elements of Office Kaizen in the face of any and all attacks. It seemed a distant memory with only a few moments of pain, but now that he was thinking about it, some of the conflicts came back to him in vivid detail.

He remembered what had happened when he had visited the Mieux operation just outside of Paris, six months into the Office Kaizen implementation. Every Biginslow location had been mandated to implement SLIM-IT by the end of June. Each site had been required to staff a full-time mentor who was then trained at one of several sites as an Office Kaizen implementer. Sites that requested additional help were directed to a consulting company that they could engage to help them. While the program and its structure had been mandated by corporate, each site was responsible for getting to the milestones in its own way. Whenever George visited a site, the first thing he asked about was Office Kaizen implementation progress.

In Mieux, it became quickly apparent that the site had been doing nothing except submitting "slightly optimistic" (as the director termed them) progress reports. Yet there was no executive steering committee, no chartered teams, no initial KCG 20 Keys assessment, and not one primary visual display board in a building with 400 people. Only a few of the work groups were having even a weekly work group meeting (which they had been having before Office Kaizen). George could accept misunderstanding, honest mistakes, misguided enthusiasm, and fear-motivated defensive reactions. That was normal resistance and the reason why firm, unabated, unyielding structure was a primary requirement for successful Office Kaizen implementation (or anything else).

Yet, the director and his staff had simply stonewalled the entire Office Kaizen effort. Bulletin boards were counted as primary visual displays, the daily work group meetings had been deemed a waste of productive time and the KCG 20 Keys were preempted by "just as good" measurements that were already being used. He could still remember his reaction. He had never felt so betrayed; he and his staff had been lied to! He knew that this was learned behavior, because most corporate-led efforts were half dead at corporate before the first follow-up site visit; and everybody was always grateful if "the program" was not mentioned. They just hadn't realized that things were different this time. He had called the entire senior staff into the main conference room at the end of the day and blasted them. He explained his disappointment. He told them that he understood that few programs in the past had endured, and they might have thought that Office Kaizen would be allowed to die an early death. This, he told them, would not occur.

He had then told them that they had eight weeks to recover and get on track with an ESC, teams, daily work group meetings, and visual displays. He told them they had an additional eight weeks after that to get the KCG 20 Keys up and running in every work group. He said that he wanted weekly progress reports with digital pictures of meetings, boards, and the like. If progress was not on track, he told them that he would return earlier than the eight weeks and take "necessary action," including the replacement of the entire management team.

Although Mieux stuck in his mind, the same sort of resistance occurred in smaller pieces everywhere. He could not believe the tenacity of some managers' resistance to change. Yet, with enough structure and nowhere to hide, almost all of the managers and supervisors in the company got onboard. Not more than two percent of the overall management ranks were let go because they could not be coached into acceptance. Sadly, one of his staff had been one of them; the individual just couldn't carry the flag and lead the implementation. Five site managers out of 110 had been involuntarily terminated because they would not or could not implement Office Kaizen. Yet, that was less than the average seven involuntary terminations for poor performance in a typical year. George knew it could have been normal statistical variability but it was his staff's belief that Office Kaizen had saved more than a few site managers who had possessed energy and good intentions but who had not known how to provide the structure for excellence.

Of course, results are where the rubber meets the road. George's most vivid memories from the first year were the kaizen blitz reports that teams would present whenever he visited a site or was invited to a headquarters out-brief. Every one of these blitz reports had been both exhilarating and frightening. The exhilaration came from seeing the sparkle in employees' eyes as they showed what three to five people could do in a week if they were given the structure and ownership. A few of the teams had discovered ways to save over $500,000 annually from improvements they had made. The average savings per event in Biginslow had been over $100,000. The corporate finance department had estimated that the over 3300 blitz events held in the company over the last two years (a little over one per month per location) had contributed a net two percent profit to the bottom line.

Yet, volume-adjusted profits in the second year had increased eight percent! There was dramatically more effective management of all types of initiatives and, at the same time, continual, increasing elimination of waste within all work groups. Most startling had been the relationship between the average KCG 20 Keys scores of work groups and their performance. With only a year and a half of data and the usual variability and unknown influences, it was still a cloudy picture but it couldn't be dismissed. Those sites with higher average scores on the KCG 20 Keys within work groups were three times more likely to be at the high end of the productivity, profit, and customer service performance curves than the lower-scoring sites. Another year or two of data would clear up that picture, but George didn't need proof. He could see the results, the employees could feel them, and his shareholders benefited from them.

George looked at his watch. It was time for the meeting. He got up from his desk and walked to the conference table. He picked a box out of a fancy gift bag containing two dozen such boxes and opened it. It was an expensive fountain pen with the new company logo. I'll put mine on now, he said, before I give them out to the board members and my staff. He slipped the pen into his shirt pocket, picked up the bag, and opened the board room door. The sunlight from the windows glinted off his pen as he entered the room; the reflection of the "Faster and More Profitable" logo flitted across the faces of the applauding board members and staff. George smiled.

Appendix A

KCG 20 Keys
of Office Kaizen

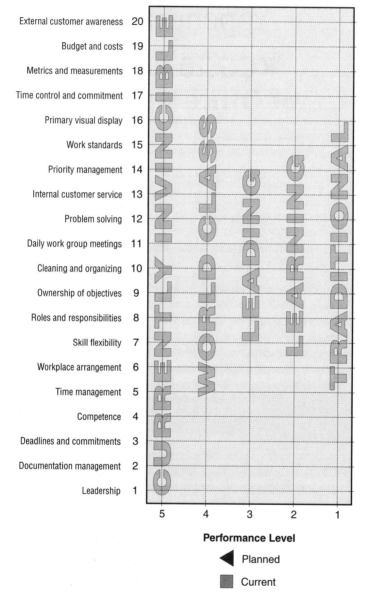

Figure A.1 Template for work group's self-assessment and annual goals.

Level	Key #1—Leadership
1	The work group has no defined leadership structure and there is no clear leader. No work area vision or goals exist.
2	The work group recognizes the group leader, and a work group vision is defined. There is little worker participation in decision making.
3	A plan to achieve objectives is developed. Associates have input to decisions, but the leader gives final approval.
4	Everyone in the work group understands the plan to achieve objectives. Decisions are made by group consensus facilitated by the leader whose main role is that of a coach.
5	Everyone understands the vision, the plan, and road map to get there. Associates are empowered to make decisions to achieve objectives. The leader/coach provides guidance when needed and his/her input is always appropriate and welcomed.

Level	Key #2—Documentation Management
1	There is no central location for work group documentation. Documentation is missing, redundant, and/or out-of-date. Associates maintain personal storage areas. There is no consistent process for document handling.
2	Elimination of outdated, redundant, and unnecessary documentation has begun. A storage area for shared documents has been established but is not always used.
3	No personal storage areas for work group documentation remain. Occasionally, documents are still misplaced, duplicated, and/or lost.
4	All associates in the work group use the central area for work group documents and very seldom is a document misplaced, and/or found to be out-of-date, or in two places at once.
5	Documents are always where they are supposed to be, and they are up-to-date and accurate. All documents are quickly available to any work group member on demand.

Level	Key #3—Deadlines and Commitments
1	Deadlines are not defined, documented, communicated, or measured. Commitments are regularly missed without accountability.
2	The work group begins to document and measure deadlines and commitments. Awareness of the need to meet commitments is built. Commitments and deadlines are still regularly missed.
3	The work group implements a structured system to manage deadlines. Commitments and deadlines are usually met, but sometimes deadlines and commitments, some major, are still missed.
4	The work group is skilled in using a structured system to manage deadlines. Ownership of every aspect of managing commitments is defined and internal/external customer satisfaction is met through consistent on-time delivery.
5	Firm schedules are always set and are never missed. Internal and external customers have full confidence that delivery will be on time, every time.

Level	Key #4—Competence
1	There may be general descriptions of functional and technical (F/T) competence requirements in the area, but they are not communicated. There is no process in place for competence improvement.
2	The work group defines F/T requirements for itself. Associates begin to improve current skill sets through training and education.
3	The work group begins measuring competence against best practices in their industry/field. All work group members attend at least three relevant inside/outside technical workshops each year.
4	Work group F/T competence is on par with the best in the industry/field. The area associates have the ability to teach F/T skills to other associates.
5	Some members of the work group conduct workshops in their industry/field and at least one is published as an F/T innovator in the industry/field.

Level	Key #5—Time Management
1	Time management is not viewed as an important tool in the work group. Overtime and/or long days are normal.
2	The work group realizes that time management is important. An efficient, consistent, and standard time management (ECSTM) system is beginning to be used in the work group.
3	All work group members use an ECSTM system with few problems. Work group members can access each other's schedules and plans. Overtime and long days occur no more than once a week.
4	All work group members use an ECSTM system expertly. Long days are rare and time is rarely wasted due to poor time management.
5	It is easy for all personnel at the site to quickly access appropriate portions of the work group members' schedules and plans. All work group members feel as if their time is always effectively used.

Level	Key #6—Workplace Arrangement
1	Workplace layout just "happens," with no planning or thought as to work flow, storage, traffic patterns, and person-to-person communication.
2	The work group begins to explore possible areas of improvement in the physical layout of their area. Work group members construct a diagram of the current layout and begin to think about alternatives.
3	The work area arrangement has been modified to improve work flow and communications. There are still some issues that have not been resolved but they are being explored.
4	Work group equipment is placed to support key processes and work flow. Workspace is flexible and highly mobile. The work group can reconfigure their area when necessary.
5	All floor space is fully utilized to maximum effectiveness. The work group members believe that they have a near-perfect arrangement to be productive without wasted space.

Level	Key #7—Skill Flexibility
1	Cross-training is not tracked, and/or it is done informally, and/or it is done only when a problem arises.
2	The work group begins to define tasks and begins to display skill flexibility charts in the work area.
3	Skill flexibility for all appropriate tasks in the work group is tracked and displayed visually. Goals for work group flexibility are established. At least 50% of the work group members are skilled in three critical tasks.
4	The work group has training plans for each member's skill development. Every task can be done by at least two work group members. At least 75% of the work group members can do all tasks in the work group. The work group is beginning to learn tasks of up/downstream work groups.
5	Except for recent hires, all work group members can do 90% of the work group's tasks. Members visually track tasks of immediately adjacent up/downstream groups and can do 50% of the tasks.

Level	Key # 8—Roles and Responsibilities
1	Roles and responsibilities (R&R) are left to evolve on their own or are assumed on the basis of past work practices.
2	A member of management, without any discussion, specifies R&R for each work group member.
3	The supervisor or leader of the work group meets individually with each group member to jointly develop the member's specific R&R.
4	Through group brainstorming and discussion by the entire group, each person's specific R&R are negotiated and defined in detail.
5	Level 4 above *and* all R&R are continually monitored and modified as required through discussion among the work group members.

Level	Key #9—Ownership and Objectives
1	There is no clear ownership of objectives in the work group, and/or objectives continually change and evolve on their own.
2	The work group identifies and displays short-term (daily and weekly) goals with milestones, completion dates, and accountabilities (MCDA). Medium-term goals (monthly and quarterly) are being added to the visual display.
3	Short- and medium-term goals are displayed and tracked with MCDA. The group quickly deals with occasional missed goals. Plan changes create some problems.
4	Short-, medium-, and long-term (annual to several years) goals are tracked and displayed with MCDA. The work group is totally accountable for objective attainment and adjusting to changes. Almost no problems exist.
5	The work group has full ownership for all objectives, handles changes easily, and adjusts proactively to potential problems. Objectives are always met.

Level	Key #10—Cleaning and Organizing
1	Open space and storage is cluttered with excess and unused equipment, supplies, and papers. There is visible grime, obvious trash (old newspapers, copy machine rejects, etc.), and dust in the work area.
2	A formalized plan to improve C&O is being developed. Obvious trash is removed by the end of each day by work group members. Unused equipment and out-of-date materials, supplies, and files (MSF) have been removed.
3	C&O performance is assessed at least twice per week with checklists and visually displayed and reviewed results. MSF are labeled in both the work area and storage areas.
4	Work group members conduct C&O activities during the day. Audits show near-perfect C&O performance. Only rarely is an item out of place. Members begin to plan for optimum placement of MSF.
5	99.99% C&O performance exists. Work area MSF are stored, labeled, and arranged for optimum ease of use.

Level	Key #11—Daily Work Group Meetings
1	No daily work group meetings (DWGM) are held or they are only held when there is special news (for example, merger, reorganization, and so on).
2	DWGM have begun but are not attended by all work group members. Some meetings are missed and some meetings seem pointless.
3	DWGM are held almost every day and are attended by most work group members. Efforts are underway to make the DWGM relevant to all group members.
4	DWGM are held every day, without exception. Attendance is 100% and most work group members participate actively.
5	Every work group member views the DWGM as an essential and critical element of the job.

Level	Key #12—Problem Solving
1	The work group has few or no "team tools" that everyone understands for manipulating data and/or identifying/solving problems.
2	A majority of the work group members understand a few tools but they are applied inconsistently. A plan is developed to identify necessary tools and teach them to the work group.
3	All work group members understand a small set of basic problem-solving tools. The proper tools are used for significant problems, but there is still much "subjective" analysis of minor problems.
4	All work group members understand and apply appropriate tools for all problem solving. Tool usage skills are tracked on cross-training displays.
5	The work group members (except new hires) are expert in all of the basic tools that might be used in the work group. Additional skill development plans are always in process.

Level	Key #13—Internal Customer Service
1	The quality of service to other areas is poor and there are no measurement system and improvement plans in place.
2	Work group asks other areas to measure their performance. Issues are identified and displayed for improvement planning. Many problems still exist.
3	Metrics are in place and displayed to formally monitor customer satisfaction. Continuous improvement plans are defined to address root causes of the most serious problems. Small problems occur regularly but are dealt with quickly.
4	All major and many minor root causes of customer dissatisfaction have been eliminated. Almost all potential problems have been proactively eliminated.
5	Customers' satisfaction is near perfect. Satisfaction metrics are consistently at the very top.

Level	Key #14—Priority Management
1	The work group functions via crisis management. Environment is purely reactionary as members are only fighting fires.
2	Work group priorities are imposed on the group. There is some discussion within the group as to how they must meet the priorities, but most decisions are made by some level of management.
3	There is a good level of work group discussion involved in deciding how to meet imposed priorities. The work group begins to set many of its own priorities and develops and displays plans to manage them.
4	The work group begins to take ownership of all of its priorities and develops and displays plans for them. Management reviews and approves the work group's plans but seldom makes any changes.
5	The work group develops all of its own priorities after being given broader organization priorities. The work group priorities are 100% in line with organization priorities and need no management approval.

Level	Key #15—Work Standards
1	There are few standardized work procedures (step-by-step instructions, flowcharts, lists of needed data/forms, approximate time required) that are known by and/or accepted by the work group.
2	All work group members are familiar with what a good work standard would look like. A few activities have work standards that all group members have reviewed.
3	80% of the work group's primary tasks have work standards and they are used in cross-training activities.
4	All critical activities and most minor activities (95% of the group's tasks) have standards that the entire work group helped develop, understands, and uses.
5	Standards for all work group activities have been established and the work group continually strives to improve them.

Level	Key #16—Primary Visual Display
1	There is no primary visual display (PVD), which is a large display in the work area showing the work group's status, metrics, tasks, priorities, and so on, and/or the PVD is not updated regularly.
2	The work group has a PVD and it displays information that is important to the group. The information that is displayed is kept up-to-date most (80%) of the time.
3	The work group PVD is comprehensive and has been extensively improved by work group members. The information is almost always up-to-date (95% of the time).
4	The PVD contains almost every critical element that the work group must track. Work group members have most of the responsibility for keeping the PVD up-to-date. It is current better than 99% of the time.
5	The PVD display and the performances it tracks are viewed by the work group as the heart and soul of their pride and commitment.

Level	Key #17—Time Control & Commitment
1	Work group members don't always arrive promptly and there is considerable (5% to 10%) absenteeism on occasion. Turnover in the work group is high.
2	Attendance is charted and displayed.
3	Work group members generally arrive on time. People will work late when it is required unless personal commitments are pressing. Absenteeism is less than 3%.
4	Work group members always arrive on time. Absenteeism is less than 2%. Annual turnover (not counting promotions) is less than 5%.
5	Workers are prompt, enthusiastic, and willing to work late on those rare occasions when it is required. Absenteeism is less than 1% and turnover less than 3%.

Level	Key #18—Metrics & Measurement
1	There is little or no measurement of critical processes within the work group.
2	Initial efforts are underway to identify key performance indicators (KPI) for critical processes in the work group.
3	The work group tracks and displays KPI for all critical processes and has developed and displayed plans for improvements.
4	The work group tracks and displays the KPI of all major and most minor processes as well as progress against plans for improvements.
5	The KPI of all appropriate processes are monitored on a continuous basis and corrective action is seamlessly integrated into the work group's daily activities.

Level	Key #19—Budgets and Costs
1	Budgets and cost tracking (B&CT) for the work group do not exist and/or are unknown to work group members.
2	Work group costs are displayed to the work group. Periodically (at least quarterly), work group performance against budget is reported and posted.
3	The work group budget is established at year start and posted. Performance against budget is posted monthly and the work group contributes to discussions as to how to resolve major discrepancies.
4	The work group participates in development of its annual budget. Performance is tracked and displayed and the work group is primarily responsible for budget performance with management approval/review.
5	All aspects of cost and budget development and performance are the responsibility of the work group with only minimal management coaching.

Level	Key #20—External Customer Service
1	The work group has little or no knowledge of who the external customers (EC) are and/or how the work group's efforts impact EC.
2	EC data relevant to the work group's performance are posted in the work group and reviewed and discussed. Work group begins to make plans to address the most critical issues.
3	The work group has a posted plan with milestones, completion dates, and accountabilities (MCDA) for dealing with all major EC issues. Many major issues have been resolved.
4	All major EC issues have been resolved and the work group is addressing the minor issues with posted plans that have MCDA.
5	The work group has corrected all EC issues and can resolve any new issue under its control within 24 hours. EC view the work group as a world-class unit.

Glossary of Important Terms

balanced scorecard: A technique in which a small number of measurements is used by a person or group to assess the status of all or part of an organization's performance.

blitz: See "kaizen blitz"

blitz administration team: A permanent team (with rotating members) of cross-functional employees reporting to the executive steering committee. This team is responsible for the planning, administration, presentation, and follow-up of all kaizen (or continuous improvement) blitzes held at the site. This team does not "do" the blitzes. See "kaizen blitz."

champion: A member of a site senior management team who acts as a mentor, advisor, and coach to a small team of employees that is assigned to work on a specific issue.

change team: A small group of employees (two to nine) that is assigned (typically not full-time) to work on a specific issue for a specified time period and which reports weekly to the executive steering committee. These teams are the primary engine that Office Kaizen uses to implement large improvements/changes.

charter: A written set of objectives, critical success factors, activities, deliverables, responsibility matrices, schedules, and so forth, that is developed through negotiation between the executive steering committee and a change team and is used by a change team to guide its work. See "change team" and "executive steering committee."

continuous improvement: See "reengineering."

daily work group meeting (DWGM): A tightly facilitated, loosely scripted, structured, daily, stand-up meeting held by members of an intact work group in front of the group's primary visual display and lasting no more than 10 minutes. See "intact work group" and "primary visual display."

discipline waste: The loss of productivity created by a failure of the organization to provide support at any level for a set of rules, expectations, reinforcements, rewards, leadership, and social pressures that concentrates on world-class performance.

design of experiments (DOE): A set of advanced statistical tools that determines which inputs in a situation are most influential on outputs. First transformed from the pure statistical world into a more easily used set of "cookbook" procedures by the Japanese engineer Genichi Taguchi. See "Shainin methods" and "statistical process control."

enterprise software: Often called enterprise information systems (EIS), these are software systems that attempt to merge all (or some selected portions) of an organization's data systems, reporting, and analysis into a single, integrated entity so that timely, accurate, real-time data can be effectively used by various levels of management.

executive steering committee (ESC): The senior management team of a site (or a subset of it; more than eight or nine people can be a problem) that is leading change efforts with chartered change teams. See "change team" and "charter."

focus waste: The loss of productivity created by anyone in the organization not understanding exactly what he/she should be attempting to improve upon in daily work in order for the site to attain its objectives.

intact work group: A small group (less then 10 or so) that works in close physical proximity on like or similar tasks for most of the workday. These work groups are the basic building blocks upon which the small continuous improvement element of Office Kaizen is based.

integrated product development (IPD): A loosely organized body of tools that attempts to remove waste from the product design/development process. At its best, it functions exactly like a SLIM-IT system for a product development effort. Typically, it involves a number of ineffectual teams and a smattering of technical tools.

ISO 9000 (QS-9000): A body of standards that outlines minimum requirements for basic business practice. Has become a required certification for many organizations as a result of pressure from customers. QS is the U.S. automotive industry version of the ISO standard.

kaizen: Term meaning "small, continuous improvement on everyone's part." The word itself comes from the Japanese words *kai* (small, little, good) and *zen* (good, change for the better). The intent is to create a work environment that focuses each worker on waste elimination as a normal part of the everyday work process.

kaizen action sheet (KAS) system: A method for capturing small improvement ideas within an intact work group. Intended to capture small, low-tech improvements within the work group.

kaizen blitz/event: A four- to five-day, highly structured and coached intense attack on waste in a process or work area by a small team.

KCG 20 Keys: A method for focusing an intact work group on the 20 most important elements of "how" it is operating vis-à-vis a world-class (or better) standard. The method provides an assessment of current status, management-determined future performance levels, and a month-to-month plan for improvement.

leadership waste: The loss of productivity created by the lack of focus, structure, discipline, and ownership at all levels of an organization.

lean daily management system (KCG's LDMS): A structured approach for providing focus, structure, discipline, and ownership for intact work groups. Consists of: 1) a primary visual display, 2) a daily work group meeting, 3) short-interval leadership, 4) a kaizen action sheet system, and 5) a KCG 20 Keys long-term improvement plan.

lean manufacturing: A name given to the overall operational system that is characterized by extensive use of standardized methods to remove surface wastes. The term was popularized to describe the Toyota Production System (TPS). See "pull."

macro-process: The name given to a group of micro-processes. Examples include "processing a purchase order" to "annual planning."

mega-process: The name given to a very large collection of smaller processes. Examples include "engineering," "purchasing," and "the New York processing center."

mentor: A highly skilled, extensively trained employee who coaches and facilitates all aspects of a site's Office Kaizen implementation on a full-time basis. He/she is on the executive steering committee of the site.

metric: In Office Kaizen, a measure that provides vital information about important issues, the status of ongoing efforts, and progress (or lack of it) to a person or group who can significantly impact the measure through direct, hands-on, micro-process efforts.

micro-process: The inputs, events, and outputs manipulated by a worker such as "completing an invoice."

Office Kaizen: The body of knowledge, leadership behaviors, and the social/organizational reality that create an environment in which every employee at every level is provided with the focus, structure, discipline, and ownership required to generate continuous improvement, commitment, pride, and enthusiasm to help the organization excel.

Office Kaizen waste: The 26 specific types of waste that can occur in an office or administrative environment.

ownership waste: The loss of productivity that occurs when the organization does not create a set of rules, expectations, reinforcements, rewards, leadership, and social pressures that permits employees to exert control over appropriate aspects of their activities so that they may feel pride when they make positive changes.

poka-yoke: Poka-yoke is "error proofing" (from the Japanese in which *poka* is an inadvertent error and *yokeru* is the infinitive for "to avoid"). It involves techniques (such as checklists and templates) designed to lower the probability of defects or errors.

primary visual display: A large, permanent bulletin board that operates as a daily status and improvement planning display for a single intact work group. See "lean daily management system (LDMS)."

project management: A loosely organized body of tools and techniques employed to remove waste from the management of an initiative. At its best, it functions much like a chartered change team reporting to an executive steering committee. Typically, it is much less structured and/or dependent in large part upon complex scheduling software. See "change team," "charter," and "executive steering committee."

pull: A production system in which material moves to the next station only when the next downstream process asks for it. First developed by Toyota and thus often called the Toyota Production System (TPS). Synonyms are flexible, cellular, synchronous, and just-in-time. One-by-one is a pull system in which one item at a time moves.

QS-9000: See "ISO 9000."

reengineering: A name given to a loosely organized body of tools and methods that is used to redesign processes with the intent of making radical, stretch improvements. Applies tools such as flowcharting, value stream mapping, the seven quality control tools, and the like. At its best, functions like the executive steering committee–change team system. See "change team," "executive steering committee," "seven quality control tools," and "value stream mapping."

seven quality control tools: A group of seven "simple" statistical and pre-statistical tools: Pareto charts, run charts, scatter plots, frequency distributions, statistical process control charts, cause-and-effect diagrams, and histograms. See "statistical process control."

Shainin methods: A set of advanced statistical tools that determines which inputs in a situation are the most influential on outputs. Identical in its statistical foundation to DOE. The late Dorian Shainin's approach requires extensive "testing" of assumptions prior to statistical activities in order to focus on the most important elements. See "design of experiments" and "statistical process control."

short-interval leadership: The process whereby a work group's leader visits each work group member several times a day to "see how things are" and collect critical metric data and/or provide encouragement.

Six Sigma: A process improvement methodology that relies on problem solving and statistical methods that range from the very simple (see "seven quality control tools") to the very complex (see "design of experiments"). Uses martial arts terms (for example, "Blackbelts") to describe various levels of expertise of its practitioners.

SLIM-IT: The acronym for Structure, Lean daily management system, Mentoring, Metrics, Tools, Teamwork, Training, and Technology (SLMMTTTT). This conceptual model assumes that most organizations have "enough" of the TTTT on hand to get most anything done if they can be compelled to work together by the other elements of the model.

standard work: A precise, step-by-step description of an activity, including work times and materials and information required. Serves as a basic level of acceptable performance and a training guide for new employees.

statistical process control (SPC): A set of methods for analyzing process outputs via measures of central tendency (averages, modes, and so on) and dispersion (ranges and standard deviations). Highly stylized graphs, called SPC charts, are often used to display results and study patterns.

structure waste: The loss of productivity created when the organization at any level does not create a set of rules, expectations, reinforcements, rewards, leadership, and social pressures that concentrates on world-class performance.

surface waste: Work or assets that do not add value to a product or service in the eyes of an "all-knowing" customer.

value stream mapping: A structured process-mapping technique that focuses on locating and assessing hands-on work time (cycle time) and waiting (lead) time (as well as other elements of interest). Typically involves the development of an "as is" value stream, a "to be" future state design, and an action plan of some sort to begin moving from the "as is" to the "to be."

visual system: An approach in which the condition and status of every relevant element of a work environment, as well as critical needed actions, is openly displayed and updated so that everyone knows what to do and when to do it. See "primary visual display."

waste: See "focus waste," "leadership waste," "Office Kaizen waste," "ownership waste," "stucture waste," and "surface waste."

Index